We've gone to Spain

If you want to know how . . .

Buy to Let in Spain
How to invest in Spanish property for pleasure and profit

Starting & Running a B&B in France
*How to make money and have fun running your
own chambres d'hotes*

Knowing the Law in Spain
A legal guide for visiting, living and investing in Spain

How to Buy a Home in Spain
The complete guide to finding your ideal property

Going to Live on the Costa del Sol

howtobooks

Please send for a free copy of the latest catalogue to:

How To Books
Spring Hill House, Spring Hill Road, Begbroke,
Oxford OX5 1RX, United Kingdom
email: info@howtobooks.co.uk
www.howtobooks.co.uk

REVISED AND UPDATED SECOND EDITION

TOM PROVAN

We've gone to Spain

howtobooks

To Julian

With grateful thanks to Julian who has tolerated all my frustrations while writing this book and to all my many friends in the UK and in Spain who have shared their experiences, frustrations and knowledge, making this book possible.

I would also like to acknowledge the help and support of Nikki Read of How to Books and Bill Antrobus of Deer Park Productions.

Published by How To Books Ltd,
Spring Hill House, Spring Hill Road, Begbroke,
Oxford OX4 1RE, United Kingdom.
Tel: (01865) 375794. Fax: (01865) 379162
email: info@howtobooks.co.uk
www.howtobooks.co.uk

ISBN 13: 978 1 84528 080 2
ISBN 10: 1 84528 080 6

First edition 2004
Second edition 2006

British Library Cataloguing in Publication Data.
A catalogue record for this book is available from the British Library.

Produced for How To Books by Deer Park Productions, Tavistock
Typeset by Kestrel Data, Exeter
Cover design by Baseline Arts Ltd, Oxford
Illustrations by Nickie Averill
Printed and bound by Cromwell Press Ltd, Trowbridge, Wiltshire

NOTE: The material contained in this book is set out in good faith for general guidance and no liability can be accepted for loss or expense incurred as a result of relying in particular circumstances on statements made in this book. Laws and regulations are complex and liable to change, and readers should check the current position with the relevant authorities before making personal arrangements.

Contents

TAKE MORE OF YOUR MONEY WITH YOU – WITH CURRENCIES DIRECT

If you're moving to Spain it's likely that the last thing on your mind is foreign exchange. However, exchange rates are constantly changing and as a result can have a big impact on the amount of money you have to start your new life there.

For example, if you look at the euro during 2005 you can see how this movement can affect your capital. Sterling against the euro was as high as 1.5124 and as low as 1.4086. This meant that if you had £200,000 you could have ended up with as much as €302,480 or as little as €281,720, a difference of over €20,000.

To ensure you get the most for you money it's a good idea to use a foreign exchange specialist. As an alternative to your bank, a specialist is able to offer you extremely competitive exchange rates, no commission charges and lower (if any) transfer fees. This can mean considerable savings on your transfer when compared to using a bank.

Buying Options

Spot Deal – This is the *Buy now, Pay now* option and will give you the best rate available right now and guarantee it.

Forward Contract – This is the *Buy now, Pay later* option and allows you to fix a rate for anywhere up to 2 years in advance.

Limit Order – You set the rate that you want and the market is then monitored. As soon as that rate is achieved the currency is purchased for you.

Information provided by Currencies Direct.
www.currenciesdirect.com   Tel: 0845 389 1729
Email: info@currenciesdirect.com

Preface

The weather is probably one of the first reasons that would make anyone choose to relocate to Spain or in our case to the Costa del Sol. Moving to Spain is a way to escape the often interminable grey skies of Northern Europe to a part of the world that has more than 320 days of sunshine every year. Of course it would be foolish to say that it doesn't rain in the south of Spain, but when it does you always know that the sun will soon return. In fact it may even return later the same day.

Other major reasons for moving to Spain include enjoying a better quality of life. A life free of the frustrations of the big city with people milling around under the pressure of business today and the stresses of modern life. A life where air quality is better. In fact the Mediterranean coast of Southern Spain is classified by the World Health Organisation as one of the healthiest regions of the world for air quality. Spain is also an area where the pace of life is much more relaxed.

But what is it like to go through the experience?

In this book I describe how my partner and I made our decision and how we carried it out. In doing so I also describe the experiences, frustrations and actions of two fairly ordinary individuals for whom costs and potential future costs were, and will continue to be, important. We were going into a semi-retired state earlier than planned and long-term costs needed to be considered. It is very easy for the rich to move from country to country, but when a tight budget has to be taken into consideration things can change dramatically.

This is not a book about an alternative lifestyle or an idyllic return to nature – we are too old for that. Nor is it meant to be a thorough practical guide to take the reader through the entire relocation process – there are other books and publications which do this in far more detail. Rather it describes how two people traded a familiar suburban lifestyle in Britain for a fairly similar lifestyle in Spain. It is, however, a lifestyle with a difference.

You will learn from our real life experiences. In addition, I hope that you will find, interspersed with our experiences, useful information which will help you to make the right decision.

Any decision to move from one country to another must never be made lightly. Even moving within the European Union, there are cultural and lifestyle differences which will inspire or may frustrate. Living on the Costa del Sol is inspiring overall, but when frustrations occur, they are very tiresome. Equally, some frustrations can end up having a humorous overtones.

You will find all this in the following pages . . .

Tom Provan

1

Making the Decision

Why should anyone make the decision to sell up totally in the United Kingdom and move lock, stock and barrel (and in our case dog as well!) to the most southerly part of Spain?

OUR DECISION

In our case the decision was very simple. My partner, Julian and I have shared our lives for 30 years. Suddenly we found ourselves in a new, and I suppose unexpected situation and we had to take practical decisions which would have long-term effects.

Julian had worked for 26 years for a major retail chain in the UK but at the age of 55 he was offered redundancy. On arrival at work one morning he was invited into his manager's office and was made an offer he couldn't refuse: a lump sum payment, together with activation of his index linked, final salary pension scheme, albeit at a reduced rate. Having reached the stage where working for this particular company was no longer fun, he quickly signed on the dotted line. In retrospect he might have been a bit hasty since he didn't consult an employment lawyer first, but these things happen.

Within a few days he found work in another department store as an assistant with no responsibilities other than serving the public, and within a further few months he was offered a job with a major airline as a customer services agent. This was a job which he absolutely loved. For Julian, life was good. He had proved that there is life after 50.

I had reached a senior position in another industry and had worked for the same company for around 12 years. The work was interesting and rewarding but the pressures of big business at the end of the 20th century led to increasing stress. At one time stress was probably the factor which had helped me to do a better job but now I started having panic attacks and all the other unhealthy symptoms of stress. This resulted in a two-month period of sickness leave for the first time in my career. Towards the end of this period senior colleagues visited me at home and basically offered me a redundancy package. Was this a way to remove an expensive member of staff and replace me with someone who would cost the company a lot less money? Is our story so far familiar?

Like Julian, perhaps I should have contacted an employment lawyer but I did not. At this stage my intention was to continue working in the same industry and I did not want to make enemies. I accepted the package. It offered me the opportunity to become self-employed – something I'd always wanted to do. I set myself up as an independent consultant within the same industry and initially most of my previous contacts made very sympathetic noises about the amount of work they would be able to offer me. Things were looking good.

Unfortunately the anticipated level of work did not materialise as quickly as I would have liked. When you leave a company it is amazing how quickly former contacts forget about you. The real problem with being self-employed as a one man band is that when you are marketing yourself you are not earning and when you are working you are not lining up the next client.

Julian and I began to realise that we had arrived at a crossroads in our life.

At this time we lived in southwest London where property prices and living costs were very high. Unexpectedly our existing careers had come to an end – an experience which unfortunately happens to many people today since jobs are no longer for life. Julian was working for the airline but as he was now 60 and I was 55 we had to think long and hard about our future. Should we try to stay in the rat race or should we consider a move to a place where life would be less stressful?

Julian had an index-linked pension. Being over 50, I could activate my pension and take a lump sum payment which would clear some liabilities such as credit card debts. Both of us had enjoyed successful careers and we had been the classic case of double income no kids – DINKYs. We had enjoyed three or four holidays a year. Whenever any new bit of technology appeared on the market we were among the first to own it. As a result our various credit cards had taken a battering over the years and we had quite high debts on them. These debts were the first things that had to go. We still had a mortgage, although nothing like the amount that a lot of my younger former colleagues had but, because we had lived in our house for 16 years there was a lot of equity in our property. If we decided to sell we should have enough money to clear all our debts and buy elsewhere without even thinking about a mortgage. As a result we would need far less income to live comfortably.

The first consideration about any move after living in the same area for so long was that we would be leaving friends whom we had known for 25 years. We decided, however, that true friends would still keep in touch no matter where we decided to move to and that anyone who did not keep in touch was probably not a very good friend in the first place. We were also fortunate not to have to think about family commitments.

Having decided that we needed to move the next decision was to where. The English countryside was a possibility. There are many very pretty villages in Britain, but the problem was the price of UK property. Pretty villages in the south of England, where the climate should be relatively pleasant, can be very expensive and the further north we might move, the less predictable the weather, particularly in winter. What would we actually achieve if we moved within the UK? The same high level of council taxes. The same weather. High property prices in desirable areas. In other words, overall high costs! A major upheaval in our lives with perhaps very few benefits.

So we began to think that perhaps we should move abroad – but where? In leaving Britain the world was almost our oyster, although if we wanted to move permanently we really had to stay within the EU.

First of all, we thought about France.
The climate in the north is very like that in the south of the UK and possibly even colder in winter so there would

be no great advantage to northern France apart from lifestyle. The south can be very expensive in the well known areas, although there are still pockets of affordable property to be found. The south west was a possibility, but at this stage in our thinking we discounted France since the actual cost of living in many parts of France is not too different to that in Britain. The only real advantage we could see to France was the fact that I speak fluent French.

Then we thought about Italy.

A wonderful climate, but the north is generally an expensive area in which to buy property and there would probably be very few desirable properties that we could afford to buy. Tuscany and the surrounding regions tend to attract the richer expatriate. The south is much cheaper but more remote. On the plus side Italy has a wonderful laid-back lifestyle and it is a very beautiful country with amazing culture and history. However, it is probably out of the reach of anyone other than the very rich. Plus there could be a language problem in the areas we could afford since neither of us speaks any Italian.

We then considered Greece.

A beautiful, charismatic country with a wonderful climate and a fascinating history but possibly we might experience problems in communication unless we learned to speak (and read) Greek. We might not even be able to read the road signs in the more remote areas. In addition, in the coastal areas where English is more widely spoken we would have to face the annual invasion of the package holidaymakers from northern Europe. That possibility did not appeal to us in the slightest.

And how about islands such as Cyprus or Malta?
Again, these have wonderful climates and English is widely spoken so communication would not be a problem. We were warned, however, that living on an island can be difficult. You are cut off from the mainland, and communication and travel can be more difficult. Your life can become very insular. Most people we know who have sampled island life eventually returned to mainland living.

The other Mediterranean islands of Sardinia, Corsica, Sicily and the Balearics were rejected for the same reasons.

Anywhere else in the world might be considered but could pose problems. We might be restricted by visa regulations to a six months per year residency permit which would be no use if we wanted to live there all year round.

Therefore for us the choice was becoming very simple. Spain, or in our case the Costa del Sol appeared to have more positives than negatives to recommend it. The Costa Blanca could have been equally attractive because of its climate. Further north on the Mediterranean coast the summers are hot but winters can be more unsettled. We did not want to have too much rain – there is enough of that in Britain.

For us, it helped that we already had friends who had made the decision to move to the Costa del Sol. We could benefit from their first-hand experiences and encouragement. In fact, since arriving here, we have met very few expatriates who would even consider going back home. Spain is now home to many people from the UK and other northern European countries. It is estimated that there are some 750,000 UK citizens living in Spain and that accounts for only those who have registered with the authorities. The real figure is probably much higher. Some have retired here. Some work from here. Some have taken jobs here, although to do that it would probably be beneficial to speak fluent Spanish. Some have bought holiday homes purely as an investment. Others have bought holiday homes with a view to using them as a permanent home in the future.

There is also the considerable benefit today that if you live within the EU, there are very few problems in moving to live in another EU country.

So, the Costa del Sol was our choice.

Initially (2001) we were surprised by the low cost of property compared to the southeast of England and the apparent overall low cost of living. We had been told that the cost of living was very low but I suppose we did not really believe it until we actually lived here. Doing our sums we realised that by cashing in our chips in London we could move to an area where our lifestyle should be better:

◆ No more rush hour commuting – packed trains, jammed motorways or congestion charging.

◆ Fewer traffic jams – although the coast road in the Costa del Sol can resemble the M25 on occasions but only in August.

◆ A more laid-back attitude to life.

◆ More sun and certainly less rain – blue drizzle rather than grey drizzle.

◆ Better quality of food. Fruit and vegetables are virtually all organically grown – you can actually buy fresh fruit and vegetables at the roadside direct from the grower. The price of organic food here is not twice as high as non-organic! The buyer does not get ripped off.

◆ A large expatriate community where, if you really must stay as British as possible, you can – although that would be to miss out on Spain and its rich culture and history.

◆ A large number of publications in English. It is easy to learn to speak a language but it can be more difficult to read it. You can even buy all the UK tabloids and broadsheets. They are now printed in Spain on a daily basis and appear on the news-stand at the same time as the local papers.

All this, plus the marvel of digital satellite television, which means you can still enjoy the benefits above without missing your favourite TV programmes in the UK!

Having lived in Spain for over two years we made one other important discovery which really affects your life. In June daylight hours are 7 am to 10 pm while in December it is daylight from 8.30 am until almost 7 pm. No more putting the lights on at four in the afternoon and virtually no chance of Seasonal Affective Disorder – no more SAD!

Now I've explained how we made our decision here are a few practical points that might help you make yours.

PRACTICAL POINTS

Do you want to live in Spain all the time? If so, do you want (or even need) to keep a property in your home country?

If you intend to rent out your UK property, the problems of being an absentee landlord can be immense. Most experienced landlords know that many long-term rentals involve total redecoration with all its costs whenever the tenants change. Arranging this from a distance can be more difficult and expensive. As an absentee landlord you will need to employ a property management company and this will cost you money.

We had many friends who asked, 'Why don't you keep the UK property and rent it out?' For us there was an easy answer – we needed to sell in the UK in order to fund the purchase of property in Spain and we certainly did not want to rent in Spain or have a mortgage. We considered ourselves too old to take out new mortgages. For anyone with sufficient money it would be a better bet to buy a second property in Spain and be a local landlord. At least you can keep an eye on the second property without using an agent.

Other friends said, 'Why don't you keep the UK property? The capital appreciation will be greater.' Once more there is a strong counter argument. Property prices on the Costa del Sol have risen in the last few years at a similar (or higher) rate to those in the UK (so long as you bought the right property). Just as in the UK, the paramount factor is location, location, location – more of that in a later chapter. Of course there is always the possibility that property prices will stop rising or even fall but this could happen in any country. In our case the value on paper of the first property we bought in Spain rose by 95 per cent in two years while our second property rose by 31 per cent in one year.

*If you are worried about healthcare should you move
permanently to Spain?*
I will resolve any worries you might have about
healthcare in a later chapter?

*Are you worried about the potential distance between
you and your friends and family back in the home
country?*
You needn't be since travel between Malaga or
Gibraltar and the UK is probably quicker than from
London to Manchester by train or car. With
increasing competition between airlines for business
it is probably even cheaper than the train in the UK.
One of our friends here wanted to go back to the
West Country and bought a return flight to Bristol
for £100 since she wanted to avoid paying the
train fare from London to Bristol which was around
£80!

What about coping with the climate?
Believe it or not the climate is not difficult to cope
with. Yes, it can be very hot in July and August but
only into the 90s normally and there is very low
humidity. This is a small price to pay for winter
temperatures which rarely go below 50°F. The secret
in coping with the climate is to buy the right property
in the right position, but more of this later when I
talk about choosing the ideal property. Many

new properties are built with air conditioning but if you buy sensibly it is really not necessary. After all, the local inhabitants of the Costa del Sol have coped without air conditioning for centuries using common sense.

Will I have problems with communication?
Almost certainly not! A working knowledge of Spanish is not difficult to develop and I believe that it is only polite to try to do this. However business transactions – banks, lawyers, doctors, insurance, building work – can all easily be carried out in English. The only people who may have problems in day-to-day living are those who choose to relocate to a remote part of the countryside. For them a good working knowledge of the language would be a real advantage. Living in the country, however, you would find that you pick up the language very easily. Spanish is not a difficult language to learn.

I hope this section has answered some of your questions and given you further food for thought. For us we knew after the first year that the decision to move from the UK was the right one.

2

Choosing a Location

Having made the decision to move to Spain the next
step is to choose the location for your dream home and
consider the types of property you might be offered. The
secret to success in buying the right property is the right
research. And in every country the main consideration is
location, location, location.

Spain is a huge country with vast areas of open unspoiled
land and a wonderful heritage. It is much bigger than the
UK and the population is about the same. The choice of

location can be bewildering. If you are not sure about your choice of region buy a good guide book to Spain and read it very carefully so that you can narrow your search to several distinct areas of the country. Having selected the area it then makes sense to rent a property there so that you can look for your final purchase.

Currently there are more than a million foreign property owners in Spain and that is only counting those who have registered with the authorities. The majority live around the Mediterranean coastline with very few living inland. We chose the Costa del Sol, or more accurately the western end of the Costa del Sol, but that may not be right for you. However, your experience will be similar wherever you choose to move.

I will describe later why we made our decision on location but before I do, I will assume that, like us, you will want to live close to the sea and take you on a tour of the Costas of Spain from North to South – to help you make your decision.

THE COSTA BRAVA
Just across the French border the **Costa Brava** is a wild rugged coastline of immense natural beauty which in the northern part (just over the French border) is particularly unspoiled and is likely to remain so. Here the mountains tumble into the sea and there is very little room for development of any sort. The commercial Costa Brava or

Costa Dorada a bit further south has some of the old ugly holiday sprawls such as **Blanes, Lloret de Mar** and **Tossa** which date from the sixties when package holidays began. There are, however, some unspoiled areas even here and beautiful fishing villages such as **Tamariu** and **Aigua Brava**. **Sitges**, south of Barcelona, is a particularly attractive resort and many foreigners live there. It is also a popular resort for Barcelonians to buy summer property. The second most popular museum in Spain after the Prado in Madrid is the Dali museum in **Figueres**, an attractive seaside town in the extreme north of the Costa Brava. Dali's home town of **Cadaques** is truly beautiful.

Inland the land rises to the foothills of the Pyrenees with many undeveloped areas. These areas are perfect should you want to be close to the sea but also within easy driving distance of the Pyrenees for skiing in the winter. Two of Spain's most interesting cities are in this area. **Girona** has an absolutely stunning mediaeval centre and really is one of the most attractive and possibly under-rated cities in Spain. **Barcelona** is chic, cosmopolitan, cultured and has some of the most stunning architecture to be found in any city in Europe, ranging from the modern architecture of Gaudi to fascinating older buildings in the Barrio Antiguo. Barcelona is probably one of the most exciting cities in Europe. Needless to say, should you have dreams of living in Barcelona property is expensive, particularly in good neighbourhoods. Generally the Costa Brave is expensive.

The other major cities in the region are **Lleida** and
Tarragona, where you will find one of the largest theme
parks in Europe, Port Aventura, now owned by Universal
Studios.

Further south the coastline flattens out around **Tarragona**
to form the **Costa Dorada**, which stretches all the way to
the **Ebro Delta** – a paradise for bird watchers. The entire
coastline is in the province of **Catalonia** a region of Spain
which would like to be independent. In fact the first
language of Catalonia is Catalan and many locals will only
speak Castillian Spanish to foreigners. Many inhabitants
of this region are bilingual, but their two languages are
Catalan and Castillian so there can be occasions when
English is not spoken, particularly in country areas.

Climate

The climate on the Costa Brava and the Costa Dorada
offers summer temperatures which are rarely too high,
but it can be humid with 20 to 31 inches of rain per
year (500–800 mm). Winters are mild on the coast
but can be very harsh inland because of the mountains.
Thunderstorms are also quite common because of the
proximity of the Pyrenees. It is not the choice of those
who want year-round sunshine, but if you want sun in the
summer and ski resorts in the winter it could be an ideal
choice for your home.

Communications

Catalonia has excellent connections with the rest of Spain

and with France. There is an extensive rail network and there are also high speed trains from this region to other parts of Europe. There is a good motorway system and there are major airports at Girona and Barcelona.

Property

Property prices have a very wide range in Catalonia. The cities are expensive and the coastal regions vary from very expensive on the Costa Brava (since there is very little room for building on a large scale) to much more reasonable on the Costa Dorada. I have to say that overall this area is much more expensive than the rest of Spain and for very good reasons.

THE COSTA BLANCA AND THE COSTA DEL AZAHAR

These two Costas are in the province of **Valencia**. The land immediately next to the coast is low lying and has many dunes and sandbars off shore which enclose lagoons. These help to keep the coastal plain fertile and the region is famous for its citrus harvest. There are many well-known resort areas including **Calpe**, **Denia**, **Benidorm** (infamous for its high-rise blocks) and **Javea** which has a huge expatriate community. All these resorts are in the province of **Alicante**. The main towns of the region are **Valencia**, which is a large industrial and commercial centre, **Alicante** and **Castellon**.

There is a range of mountains running parallel to the

coast in which you can find interesting hill villages which offer panoramic views of the coast.

Property

Property on the Costa Blanca and the Costa del Azahar is cheaper than on the Costa del Sol and there are many developments of bungalow style villas and apartments at reasonable prices. The building density can be quite high in places – that is what keeps property prices relatively cheap. There are many companies that organise property exhibitions in the UK featuring villas and apartments for sale on the Costa Blanca. Needless to say, most of these properties are being sold off-plan – more about this in Chapters 3 and 4. The one town here which seems to be in the process of being taken over by the British is **Torrevieja**, one of the largest building sites in Europe. However, in many of the other resort areas here you may also find yourself living in England in the sun.

Climate

Leisure and sports facilities are good but if you are looking for golf courses you need to look further south towards the Costa del Sol. The climate is Mediterranean with hot summers and mild winters and an average of 320 days sunshine a year – similar to the Costa del Sol. The WHO also recognises the climate and the air quality in this part of Spain as being among the healthiest in the world.

Communications

Communications between Valencia and the rest of Spain are very good, with modern motorways and railways together with major airports at **Alicante** and **Valencia**. Since the region is not a major business area the number of scheduled flights is lower than to other areas but there is a healthy presence of charter and low-cost airlines to take care of your travel needs throughout the year.

THE COSTA CALIDA

The Costa Calida is in the extreme south-east corner of Spain in the province of **Murcia**. The main towns of the region are **Cartagena**, **Lorca** (thought by some to be the prettiest town in the area) and the capital, **Murcia**.

Property

The region is largely undeveloped and not very well known, although there are some very good beaches and resorts such as **Aguilas**, **Mazarron** and **Mar Menor**. The Costa Calida is unlikely to be a first choice region for someone planning to live in Spain long term.

Climate

The region is primarily agricultural and has a Mediterranean climate with hot summers and mild winters. One up-market development on the Costa Calida is the **La Manga** Club resort – an exclusive sports and leisure development on the Mar Menor lagoon.

Communications

Communication with the rest of Spain is quite poor since the rail service only goes as far as Valencia or Alicante. There are airports at **Almeria** and **Murcia** but they tend to be served by seasonal charter flights. The only consolation is that due to the lack of development, property prices remain fairly low on the Costa Calida. Prices are, however, rising and **La Manga** is already very expensive.

> If I have traveled down the east coast of Spain rather quickly, I apologise. The experiences I describe concern our move to the Costa del Sol, but you might find you prefer other parts of this wonderful coastline. Should any of these areas appeal do please check them out before you commit yourself to a purchase – do not make a decision at a property exhibition in the UK. Visit your chosen areas before you make any decisions.

ANDALUCIA

Why did we choose to move to Andalucia?
The answer is very simple. It is the one region that sums up Spain for everyone. Andalucia is the Spain of the guide books and the tourist brochures. It is the region of sandy beaches, rugged mountains and deep gorges, white villages, spectacular historical towns and monuments,

festivals or *ferias*, flamenco, the guitar and the bullfight. It is a region rich in history dating back before the Roman invasion. There are many colourful reminders of the Moorish occupation of Spain and wonderful examples of how Christian Spain changed after the Moors were driven out.

Andalucia is the second largest region of Spain and contains many major towns and cities, some of which are tourist attractions in their own right as well as being thriving commercial areas. Among those towns and cities are **Algeciras** (the major port for Africa which is only nine miles from Spain), **Almeria**, **Antequera**, **Cadiz** (the port from which Columbus sailed to discover America), **Cordoba**, **Granada**, **Jerez** (home of sherry), **Malaga**, **Ronda** and **Seville** (the regional capital).

Some parts of the coastline are highly developed and represent the image of the Costa del Sol as seen in many holiday brochures – high-rise, high-energy with 24-hour entertainment, busy and very 'sea and sangria'. Other areas are totally unspoiled, where development is still in its infancy. In between there are areas where the development is more sympathetic and rarely stretches back more than a mile from the sea. The main resorts are described below.

The Costa del Sol stretches almost the whole length of the southern portion of Spain and begins with the **Costa Almeria**. Here tourism has left the coast practically untouched and development is minimal. For many years this part of Andalucia was largely ignored; it was thought to be a harsh landscape of sun-drenched mountains and rocky plains. Largely untouched by mass tourism, even today, this coast has many villages with less than 2,000 inhabitants. Some of these villages could be the ideal choice if you want to live in real Spain.

The area also contains the only desert in Europe, which is near the town of **Tabernas**. Film sets from the famous spaghetti westerns have been preserved here and this desert was also used as a location for the epic film *Lawrence of Arabia*.

Property prices on the Costa Almeria remain relatively low at the moment but development is beginning to take place and prices are rising.

THE COSTA TROPICAL

Our next stop on this coast is the **Costa Tropical** in the province of **Granada**. Once again this coast is less developed than the Costa del Sol itself but development is taking place, albeit sympathetically and it is certainly a growth area for the future. Development is helped by the close proximity of this coast to Malaga airport. In fact the closer you get to Malaga airport the higher the prices.

The area of Granada province which could be of interest to readers who want more of a return to nature is not on the coast but is an inland region known as the **Alpujarras**, a particularly beautiful group of mountain valleys in the foothills of the Sierra Nevada south-east of Granada itself. The area is dotted with little hill villages, winding roads, mule tracks and footpaths. This is just the area in which you might want to settle if you wish to escape the pressures of the 21st century. This is real Spain and you would need to speak some Spanish to live here.

The Alpujarras is as yet relatively undeveloped, although it is likely that more development will take place in the future; it always does in areas of great natural beauty because people want to live there. You won't find new apartments and huge villas with all the mod-cons of today but you might find that delightful farmhouse or *finca* with a bit of land on which you can cultivate your olives and lemons. You may even end up being independent of town water and mains electricity and have to depend on your own well together with solar power to generate your 12v electricity supply.

The climate is very pleasant. The summer temperatures are not as hot as those on the coast because of the altitude but it goes without saying that it is colder in the winter. In fact the higher you go, the more chance you have of seeing snow. At its most northerly point the Alpujarras are actually closer to Granada than they are to Malaga.

Should you want to experience even more remote parts of

Andalucia you could decide to go further inland to the provinces of **Cordoba**, **Granada** and **Jaen**. Here you will find typical Spanish villages and small farms or *fincas* all set in areas of incredible natural beauty. But property here can be very remote and may only have a dirt track for access. You may not have mains water or electricity but you will be living close to nature. As you are high in the mountains the climate tends to be very hot in the summer but it can snow in the winter. Property prices are very low in these regions and you can still pick up properties for renovation together with a reasonable amount of land for less than £50,000 but prices are rising.

THE COSTA DE LA LUZ

Leaving the Costa Tropical behind, I will leapfrog over the Costa del Sol proper to mention the Costa de la Luz, which is not really part of the Costa del Sol. This is Europe's most southerly coast and here the sea is the Atlantic Ocean. We are now west of Gibraltar and the wide sandy beaches are truly spectacular. However, the region is still remote.

This coast is very windy. One of the larger towns, **Tarifa**, is known as the wind surfing capital of Europe. Tarifa is also Europe's most southerly town and is so close to the coast of Morocco that you almost feel that you can touch Africa.

The coast has largely escaped the development seen

further east but this is changing. Golf courses are being built and this will bring in the tourists. Anyone who likes wild ocean vistas and the beauties of nature might like to consider the Costa de la Luz. This area is home to one of Europe's largest nature reserves, the **Coto Dõnana**, which apart from its fascinating animal and plant life is also the crossing point for many migratory birds on their way to and from Africa. It is truly a birdwatcher's paradise.

Temperatures on the Costa de la Luz are often cooler in the summer due to the ocean breezes but winter temperatures are also lower. This coast can be wild if there are Atlantic storms!

THE COSTA DEL SOL

The Costa del Sol today stretches from **Nerja**, near Malaga, almost to Gibraltar.

East of Malaga, **Nerja** and **Torrox** are developed but not overly so (yet) and the coastline is spectacular. The downside is that being close to Malaga there is a lot of tourist activity in the area during the summer months. Inland there are beautiful hill villages to explore, many of which can offer delightful village houses for those who want to live in a Spanish village without being too far from the bright lights of modern civilisation. The best-known hill village is **Frigiliana**, which has been restored so much by expat settlers that it almost

resembles a film set. Another very pretty hill village is
Tollox, while **Competa** is becoming so attractive to the
British it now boasts several British-owned estate
agents.

If any readers wish to consider Malaga itself as a choice
of destination they will find it to be a large, bustling city
and seaport which has kept its Spanish character. The
most interesting properties to be found in Malaga would
be in the historic old city. Malaga is probably the most
underrated city in Spain. It is highly cultural and was the
birthplace of Picasso. If you cannot live without the buzz
of big city life Malaga could be a good choice, although
old properties can be expensive.

The remainder of the Costa del Sol really breaks up into
two sections:

From **Torremolinos** to **Marbella** the coast is very highly
developed with many high-rise apartments and hotels in
Torremolinos and **Fuengirola**. In my opinion these two
areas represent the worst of 1960s and 1970s development
for mass tourism, but I would be the first to admit that
many readers might wish to live there. There are real
advantages:

◆ There is public transport – buses and trains – along
   this part of the coast.

◆ It is possible to live here without owning a car since

supermarkets, restaurants, bars and all the necessities of modern life can be within walking distance.

◆ The area is so developed for tourism that it is not necessary to speak Spanish. Virtually everyone speaks English. In fact it can be difficult to be understood in Spanish!

Although the coastal region is over-developed the picture changes when you move inland to villages such as **Coin** and **Alhaurin**. Around and in these villages it is still possible to find small, typically Spanish houses and small *fincas*, some of which need total renovation while some have already been sympathetically restored. The lower prices will surprise you. Closer to the coast is **Mijas**, a typical white village, or *pueblo blanco*, which has been taken over so much by residential tourism that almost the only people who speak Spanish in Mijas are the cleaners and gardeners. Mijas does, however, have spectacular views down to the sea at Fuengirola. Today, between Mijas and the sea development is extensive and the land either supports new apartment blocks, townhouses or villas or it has been transformed into yet another golf course. You will see signs the length of the Costa del Sol proclaiming it to be the Costa del Golf.

West of **Fuengirola** and **Benalmadena** the coast begins to change. From **Calahonda** the coastline begins to become less intensely developed, although the density is still high and it is still very tourist and in places, British orientated.

There are, however, some very attractive areas where the building density is not too high, such as **La Cala** and **Puerto Cabopino** which was the site of the BBC soap, *Eldorado* – in fact some of the actors still live here.

Property prices in this part of the coast cover all price ranges.

Marbella is our next stop on the Costa del Sol. Marbella, with its suburbs of Puerto Banus, Nueva Andulacia and San Pedro, is the Costa del Sol of the tourist brochures and the Costa del Sol at its most glittering. Expensive hotels, millionaires' yachts in the marinas, expensive cars, expensive restaurants and chic bars where people go to people watch, expensive golf courses and, of course, property prices to match. Marbella itself is home to some very glitzy hotels including the world famous Marbella Club where the Marbella success story started. **Puerto Banus** is the San Tropez of Spain. The yachts in the marina can be the size of small ferries while the parking spaces in the marina are filled with some of the most expensive examples of automotive engineering to be seen anywhere in the world. Surprisingly the restaurants along the harbour front are not all prohibitively expensive and it can be very pleasant to linger over a meal in the afternoon sun and watch how the rich folks live.

The developments here are extensive but since the prices are higher the purchasers have usually demanded more living space so the actual density of building is not so high. There are spectacular apartments and townhouses to be found here and even more spectacular villas standing in acres of garden. It's an ideal spot to look for that dream home if money is no object, but some of the prices being asked for property in the Marbella area are just as spectacular as the properties. For those on a more modest budget who want peace and quiet, I would suggest looking further west or in the hill villages inland from Marbella such as **Istan**, **Benahavis** and **Ojen**.

Once you have passed through the famous Marbella arch at San Pedro de Alcantara the coast road suddenly seems to become less busy (not always the case in July and August) and the density of building suddenly reduces. No longer does it appear that every available square metre of land on each side of the coast road is built on or under construction, although to be fair, there is still a lot of building – cranes are a fact of life in Spain at the moment. Suddenly from the coast road you can see the mountains behind the coast more clearly and you can actually see the sea itself. You can even see little old farmhouses and farming activities still taking place in the same way as they have done for centuries.

We are now heading to the other section of the Costa del Sol – the part stretching from **Estepona** almost to Gibraltar.

This is where we chose to settle and our reasons were many. Estepona itself is a wonderfully elegant resort town;

almost Edwardian in character. It has a beautiful broad sandy beach with many beach restaurants and yet even in the height of the summer season it is never crowded. There are a number of very good *chiringuitos* (beach restaurants) along the beach. From the beach on a clear day there are spectacular views of the Rock of Gibraltar and the coast of North Africa. Parking can become more of a problem in July and August although there is now a very large car park under the promenade with another being built. There is a fascinating old town which in 2002 celebrated its 5th centenary. Many of the village houses in the old town are being renovated and they can be turned into quite spectacular homes. Restored examples are now commanding quite high prices. To the west of Estepona there is a modern marina for private boats, but this marina also incorporates a working fishing harbour and fish market where you can see the catch being landed every day.

Estepona is a town where you feel as if people live and work all year round. This is very important for anyone planning to become a permanent resident. I certainly would not want to live in a ghost town out of season.

Estepona is not a Costa del Sol resort as seen in the holiday brochures. It does not have high rise hotels and apartment complexes, English restaurants and bars or masses of souvenir shops. Estepona is a Spanish resort, not a resort planned around the package holiday. In making our decision on where to live the key factor was that Estepona is not too large – in fact the boundary of the town itself is probably the toll motorway which is only about two kilometres from the beach. Beyond the motorway there is still wild countryside.

There is a wide choice of property in Estepona itself ranging from apartments on the seafront with spectacular sea views to developments of elegant townhouses with shared gardens and communal swimming pools. Once more there are prices to suit every pocket.

We decided that somewhere near Estepona should be our choice.

Moving down the coast towards Gibraltar there is a lot of development taking place. Many people who have lived here for years would prefer not to see new properties appearing and complain continuously about new development, but I have to say that the density is generally not too high at the moment. I have benefited from this development as it has provided me with a home and now that I have moved here I cannot deny the right of others to move to the Costa del Sol.

There is very little development which stretches more than one kilometre inland and since the hills come very close to the sea on this part of the coast a lot of the properties are on high ground or on the beach. They have a lot of space around them and there are virtually no high-rise developments. New planning permissions should only allow three stories and a ratio of 25 per cent building to 75 per cent open space, although there are developments which contravene regulations. This is Spain, after all! Improvements to the coast road and a new toll motorway a few kilometres inland have eased the traffic problems which this part of the Costa del Sol experienced before. Developments should also bring improvements to the infrastructure which in turn will provide everyone with an even better lifestyle. The local authority taxes payable on the new properties will increase the amount of funding which the local town halls will have available for improvements to the area in the future.

The next area on the coast is **Manilva**. The coastal town here is **Sabinillas**, a charming little Spanish town if you get off the main road which used to cut directly through it. It looks nothing from the main road but currently the beach promenade is being remodeled and many parts of the old town are being restored and pedestrianised. Since this town is particularly Spanish, properties here are very reasonably priced and there is a wide choice. Great improvements are in progress here and the coast road which passes directly through the town has now been moved into a tunnel underneath a pedestrianised area. The only real negative about Sabinillas is that unless you live in a high-rise apartment block there is not much in the way of views, since the town is almost entirely built on the flat coastal plain. Some visitors may consider that there is perhaps a little bit too much development of apartment blocks along the main road.

If you fancy living further inland you could consider Manilva itself. It is a typical small Spanish town high up on the hill and the administrative centre of this area. It remains very Spanish in atmosphere although there is already a sizable population of expatriates. It is not a typical *pueblo blanco* but from some parts of the town there are spectacular views of the sea and the mountains towards **Casares**. Manilva has adventurous ideas for the development of tourism in the area with plans for new hotels and a huge theme park in the hills on the other side of the new toll motorway. It looks like being a growth area.

Further inland, above Manilva, are the *pueblos blancos* of **Casares** and **Gaucin**. These spectacular hill villages are connected to the coast by good, if winding, roads and while they are typical of the region, there is a growing non-Spanish population in both towns, particularly in Gaucin. Both towns are a maze of narrow streets which are not very car friendly and small houses clinging to the steep hillsides. I would say that the towns themselves are more suited to the young and energetic! There are some beautiful villas and *fincas* in the hills around Casares and Gaucin but they do tend to be quite expensive.

Driving between Sabinillas and **Torreguadiaro**, the next town on the coast, there are 'urbanisations' of apartments, townhouses or villas on both sides of the road and it is in one of these urbanisations where we chose to make our home. Unless you live in Sabinillas itself a car would be advisable, although even here, there is still good public transport. There is a regular bus service from Malaga to Algeciras which is reliable, comfortable and cheap. We know many people who use it regularly and who swear by its dependability.

Moving on through the coastal part of this area you reach **Torreguadiaro** and two other towns close to it, **Pueblo Nuevo de Guadiaro** and **Guadiaro** itself. These three towns are built around the Guadiaro river – one of the few rivers in this region which flows all year round. Inland from **Guadiaro** are the small towns of **San Enrique** and **Tesorillo** which could be attractive propositions for property since they remain very Spanish. Property prices here are on the increase as the area is convenient for **Sotogrande**.

Beyond Torreguadiaro there is currently very little development apart from **Sotogrande**, a new resort built at the mouth of the Guadiaro river close to the world-famous Valderrama Golf Course. **Sotogrande** would not be to everyone's taste since it is very modern, very international, not very Spanish and very expensive. There are many modern apartments and townhouses around the new marina with views over the marina but they tend to be small. The villas in Sotogrande Alto are also *alto* (high) in price. They can cost millions of euros. However, if your budget stretches to it and you like sporting activities such as golf, tennis and sailing, Sotogrande could be the ideal choice for your dream home. To enjoy these activities you don't even need to go out of Sotogrande and there are plans to increase the number of polo grounds with the aim of turning this part of the Costa del Sol into the polo capital of Europe. It is undoubtedly a good area for investment and this is reflected in the amount of building which is currently taking place.

Beyond Sotogrande there is very little development apart from one new development called **Alcaidesa**. It is so new that I cannot really comment on it here. The town of **San Roque** overlooking the rock of Gibraltar could be your choice if you would like to consider a typical Spanish house in a typically Spanish town.

PRACTICAL POINTS

♦ Look at the regions that appeal to you and choose the one that suits you best.

♦ Plan your budget.

♦ Never commit yourself to a property on a short inspection trip.

♦ Definitely do not commit yourself at a property exhibition in your home country.

♦ Remember that estate agents need to sell to earn commission.

- Be very wary of 'free' inspection trips to view properties for sale. Remember there is no such thing as a free lunch. Your host needs to sell you property to justify the trip.

- If possible, avoid buying 'off-plan'. Do you really want to commit thousands of euros to an artist's impression? When buying off-plan you have no way of knowing who your neighbours might be, how much the running costs will be or whether the development will be residential or holiday homes.

- If you are uncertain about what you really want, the best advice is to rent first.

- Think very carefully about what you need – not just what you want.

- Be ruled by your head, not your heart.

As with all property purchases the ultimate deciding factor is location, location, location.

3

Finding a Property

Later in this chapter I will recount some of the
experiences we had while we were looking for potential
properties, but for the moment, if you are contemplating
a move to anywhere in Spain you should ask yourselves
the questions below.

How to choose a location

◆ Before looking at any property try to decide on the ideal location for you.

◆ Do you need to be close to local amenities so that you do not need to use a car every time you go out?

◆ Do you want views and if so, should they be of the sea or the mountains or both?

◆ Do you want peace and quiet at all times or can you live with some noise?

◆ Do you want to live in a new property or do you prefer established property?

TOWN OR COUNTRY?

For us the answers to most of these questions were fairly simple. It was not necessary for us to live right in the centre of town since we did not mind having to use a car. Town centres in Spain can be quite noisy so this could also be a problem.

ON THE BEACH?

We did want views. After all, one of the main reasons for moving from London, apart from the weather, was to have a view. We wanted to be able to see the sea and, wanting the best of all worlds, a view of hills or mountains would also be very acceptable. We considered front-line on the beach but very quickly rejected this as an option. The Mediterranean looks very quiet during the summer months. Then it is the cobalt blue sea of the holiday brochures. But it does have storms and we heard about properties which had real problems with beach erosion during previous winter storms. Any beachfront property needs to be built on solid rock which you can see at surface level. Properties built on sand where damp-proofing may only be a thick plastic membrane could suffer from damp problems in the future. We saw this at first hand. Cast your mind back to your childhood. You only need to dig down a few inches into sand and it is damp. Would you want to live in a house built on such a foundation?

Had we only wanted a holiday home, front-line beach would have been perfect, but on our budget we could not afford the type of beachfront property which would be totally secure in a storm or completely free of problems with damp.

DEEP IN THE COUNTRYSIDE?

What about a mountain view? We decided that we would like to be able to have this and if it was combined with a sea view, so much the better. We considered going right out into the country which is idyllic. We drove through miles and miles of beautiful open countryside with spectacular views on all sides. Our hearts almost took over the decision! This was a real escape from the rat race – absolute peace and quiet and no neighbours for miles.

Then, we stopped to think very carefully. Many properties we saw were beautiful or potentially beautiful but they were often at the end of a pot-holed dirt track. More often than not we were seeing the properties in lovely summer weather when the only problem is dust. But when it rains on the Costa del Sol it really does rain. The dirt track would turn into mud and then we would almost certainly need to have a four wheel drive vehicle just to reach our house.

Could we actually cope with absolute peace and tranquillity having been used to city life? Would friends come to visit or would they be afraid of the approach, particularly in the dark? Would we end up only having visitors for Sunday lunch but not at other times? Would we find ourselves driving all the way to the nearest supermarket to stock up and on returning home realise that we had forgotten the most important item and have to go back for it?

We rejected the idea of an idyllic country existence, no matter how spectacular the views. We were not ready to give up on civilisation and become dependent on well water, septic tanks and possibly even electric generators since many country properties do not yet have mains electricity. Some are just too remote and to install electricity could be prohibitively expensive since the owner has to pay for the cabling from the nearest source of power.

NEAR THE COAST?

So far we had rejected beach front and remote country properties. The choice was becoming easier but we still wanted relative peace and quiet with easy access to amenities. Therefore we decided that a home on high ground, close to the coast, with good views of sea and mountains would be ideal. But where and what type of property?

WHAT ABOUT THE NEARBY LAND?

We wanted views but we very quickly discovered that having views in Spain can be fraught with problems. We became expert at looking at properties and judging them not on what the view is today but how it could change in the future. Development on the Costa del Sol is such that any piece of land can potentially be land to build on. Readers contemplating buying should really take this to heart and make it one of the prime factors in selecting their future home. I will tell you more about our experiences in this area later in the chapter.

For every property we viewed we ultimately looked very carefully at the surrounding area. First, the property had to be right for us as a property but second, what could be built in the immediate area? The right property in the wrong location could be a long-term disaster. Did planning permission exist for future building and if so for what? Hill top properties could be a safe bet but if the land slopes away very steeply is the land stable? Even a steep mountainside is not impossible to build on. The rock can be blasted away to create a building platform if the hillside has views which could command a premium for finished property. Believe me, this is happening!

Properties on the edge of golf courses seemed like a good proposition. After all, a golf course is sacred soil on the Costa del Sol and there is no way that a golf course will ever become development land. However there is a negative to such properties. If our terrace is immediately above the 15th tee or the 17th green we will have a constant procession of golfers going past and the constant 'thwack' of club to ball while we try to sip our gin and tonics in peace.

In fact the only people we have met in Spain who are unhappy with their property are non-golfers who bought a front-line golf apartment. This option was therefore rejected. It might have been different had we played golf.

IN AN 'URBANISATION'?

We were getting somewhere. We wanted views, relative peace and quiet, closeness to amenities and proximity to the sea. On our budget it was therefore inevitable that we would have to buy on an 'urbanisation'. There was no way we could afford to buy an independent villa. An urbanisation is a community of owners who jointly control the development on which they live. A community offers just that – the opportunity to meet other people, many of whom will have made the same decision. Such developments can be villas, townhouses or apartments or a mixture of all three. They vary tremendously, as we soon learned.

Some urbanisations are almost totally holiday-orientated and we certainly did not want to live somewhere like that. We would be living here 52 weeks of the year and we did not want to find ourselves in a ghost town in the winter – but how does anyone judge what is residential and what is holiday accommodation? It is not really too difficult in an established urbanisation but it could be more difficult if you buy off-plan. If you view out of season you can see immediately how many properties appear to be occupied. You can see if you will have neighbours.

In addition, those that have multiple sports facilities, restaurants and bars are probably more likely to be holiday destinations rather than places where people live all year round. They will also be noisy late at night, particularly if the Spanish themselves holiday there since the Spanish go to bed very late. Out of season the urbanisation may appear to be quite quiet but what will it be like in July or August? A further pointer can be obtained from the state of communal swimming pools out of season. We saw some that had turned to green slime in March! Not a good sign for all year round living.

WHAT KIND OF PROPERTY?

So, having decided that an urbanisation would be our choice, the question was then where and what type of property? Individual villas on urbanisations tend to be quite small with very small gardens and built very close to the property next door. They are also more expensive than an equivalent sized townhouse or apartment.

Townhouses, in Spanish *adosada*, offer many of the advantages of an independent villa and often have a private garden as well as access to communal gardens. Some can actually be quite large and often have terraces on every floor. We looked at many townhouses and I have to say that we liked many of them but at the end of the day some had a problem – they are very vertical in design. In order to squeeze as much accommodation as possible into a narrow site they are built upwards and often have three floors. What happens when we get older and have to cope with all the stairs? At this stage we did not rule out the possibility of a townhouse if we could find the right one but after many years of living in a house we began to think that an apartment might be the ideal choice of accommodation. It would be all on one level (although we ended up with a duplex!). There would be less wasted space and rather than have a garden to look after we could turn to container gardening on the terrace, assuming we found an apartment with a large terrace with views. Our dream was to create an outdoor room. The first apartment we found appeared to meet this objective fully but it was off-plan and is the subject of one of the later case histories in the next chapter.

ORIENTATION TO THE SUN

There was one other major factor we had to take into account when buying an apartment and that was orientation to the sun. Summer in the Costa del Sol can be very hot in direct sunlight. Remember that temperatures quoted in a weather forecast are shade temperatures and are not always a true representation of how hot you will feel.

Our attention was drawn to traditional Spanish villages and towns. Narrow streets and shady courtyards afford protection from the heat of the midday sun – almost natural air conditioning. Our estate agent was very keen that if we were going to live here all year round including the summer months we should choose the right orientation to the sun. Her premise was that many Brits, starved of sun in the UK, usually want to buy an apartment which faces south. They feel that if they are going to move to the sun they must be in the sun. That is a grave mistake. Her advice to us was to copy the Spanish (and let's face it, they have much more experience of living in the sun) and choose east facing. If the main rooms of the apartment and the terrace face the morning sun we would be able to wake up to blue sky, have breakfast in the sun but never have the sun actually flood the living area with midday heat. An alternative would be to purchase an apartment with a true westerly orientation. Then we could enjoy very late afternoon sunshine and spectacular sunsets but once more our living area would never be subjected to direct midday sun.

We took her advice and we now live facing east. If we rise sufficiently early we are blessed with spectacular sunrises. We have sun on the terrace until the middle of the morning but since the terrace is covered the sun never shines directly into our living area. We have marble floors in the entire apartment and these provide almost natural air conditioning in the heat of the summer. I should, however, point out that marble floors can be very cold in the winter months and we find ourselves covering the floor with rugs in the winter.

OUR FINAL CHOICE

Suffice to say, we finally found a large duplex apartment within our price range. It has spectacular views over a lagoon-style swimming pool and sub-tropical gardens with onward views to a golf course, the mountains and the sea beyond. It also has terraces which are almost as large as the living area we had back in London. It is one kilometre from the sea on high ground so when the doors and windows are open there is almost always a breeze, even in the height of summer.

Our apartment also has one positive feature which we did not think important when we originally viewed it – a glass-fronted, woodburning stove. Log fires are by far the cheapest way to heat your Spanish home in the winter. They are also the most attractive way to generate heat. There seems to be an inexhaustible supply of good firewood in Andalucia and a visit to the log yard will result in the boot of the car being filled with logs for less than 20 euros.

Yes, we have to admit that there is building and development going on close to our apartment, but because we chose our location carefully it can never be a problem apart from the actual noise of building work. Unless we moved to the countryside far away from the coast there would always be the possibility of new building. We need a car to get to the nearest shops but that is only because we are lazy and do not like the thought of the walk back uphill.

4

Property Case Histories

THE NEW APARTMENT

It was our first inspection visit to Spain and we were
actually going to look at potential properties. It was
November 2000 and we were very excited. We had done
our homework. We had looked on the Internet to see
what type of property was available. We had contacted
local estate agents in the western Costa del Sol. We had
briefed the agents on the type of property we wished to
see. We had set up viewing trips. This was the first step
towards realising our dream.

The big agents

Day one and the first agent – a representative of one of the larger estate agents on the coast – arrived to take us on inspections of property. She had been briefed before we arrived. Overall there was not a lot to complain about but we did not really see what we wanted to see. We had asked to see properties with a view and a little bit of land if possible but we were shown new properties that were still under construction. We were shown a very beautiful apartment which did have a spectacular view towards Gibraltar and North Africa but it was £40,000 above our budget. Apparently the owner was keen to sell and would take an offer but would they take an offer £40,000 lower than the asking price? I think not! Not a very successful day but after all, we thought, 'Tomorrow is another day.'

Day two and the second agent representing an even bigger agency on the coast arrived to take us on a viewing trip in a very large four wheel drive vehicle. This agent must be making money! He had not really done his homework at all despite our brief. He did not even seem to know where he was going in this part of the coast. Most of the properties we saw were totally unsuitable for our needs and did not meet our brief but he did take us to a new development which on first sight met all our requirements.

We were taken round the show apartment, which looked wonderful. We were shown the quality of finish, which looked very high. We took home the lavish brochure showing an artist's impression of the development which appeared to have the Mediterranean lapping at the foot of the garden – we knew this was not the case since the sea was on the other side of the main road with another development in between, but at that time we could overlook this. We were viewing everything through rose-tinted spectacles.

The following two days were spent with local agents around the Estepona area and while some of the properties could have been suitable there was nothing which really excited us. One local agent did show us a very nice small duplex apartment which he said would be an ideal purchase as a first buy so that we could be on site to find the final property. When this happened we could either treat the first apartment as an investment for holiday rentals or sell it, which would not be too difficult. We did not listen to his advice at that time!

Making the decision

We flew back to the UK, compared all the properties we had seen and decided that while it did not match our original brief we liked the new development we had been shown. Perhaps we were trying to make a decision too quickly.

We decided that there were two properties on the plan which attracted us. Both were large two-bedroom apartments with huge terraces and views from high ground over the entire bay of Estepona all the way to

Marbella. Each apartment was described as a garden apartment with a private garden and parking space. The site office had already told us that completion was scheduled for September 2001. This was the perfect time scale for our planned removal to Spain. The agent went around and advised us on which apartment would have the better view and we took a decision to buy one of these apartments. We appeared to have found our ideal apartment: the right accommodation, a huge terrace, a private garden, spectacular views and the right price. We arranged to pay the initial deposit by credit card, so easy to do nowadays.

We then proudly showed friends in the UK the brochure, the floor plans and the descriptions of the apartment. We transferred funds to pay the pre-contract of sale deposit and found ourselves a Spanish lawyer. Everything was going so well and we were very happy with our choice. The legal proceedings went ahead and we arranged to go to Spain in late January 2001 to sign the *escritura* (the title deed) and take things forward to the next stage.

Legal problems

In our lawyer's offices late one evening in January we went through the document we were supposed to sign. The apartment had a private garden. It was not on the *escritura*! Phone call to the developers:

'Oh, that is a mistake. It should be there.'

The completion date for the property had been quoted as September 2001 but we were now told that completion would be 15 months from the date on which we signed the current document – March 2002! We were not prepared to accept this and felt that we had been deluded. Another call to the developer:

'We can negotiate late finishing penalty clauses.'

Anyone buying off-plan should do this but many do not.

We were going to pay cash and did not want a mortgage. We then discovered that the costs of building were being underwritten by a large Spanish banking group who were offering guaranteed mortgages on each property. Since we did not want a mortgage we would have to pay the cancellation fee on the agreed mortgage.

No way were we going to pay this! We had never asked for a mortgage in the first place.

And finally, whenever a builder in Spain buys land and then builds on it the value of the land is potentially higher therefore there is a tax, the *plusvalia*, to be paid on this increased value. The developer wanted us to pay this tax, to which our answer was another resounding 'No'.

We were desperately unhappy about the way things had gone and we were not prepared to sign any further documents on this property. We felt tricked by the developers and we asked our lawyer to tell the developers that we were canceling the purchase because of misrepresentation by the selling agents. He managed to get our deposit back for us, although this does not happen on every occasion.

Resist buying off-plan

This is a classic example of why I believe you should resist buying off-plan. The apartment we intended to purchase was still unfinished nine months after September 2001. There is in fact a private garden now (the *escritura* was not wrong), but the spectacular view we would have enjoyed of the bay of Estepona has now been partly blocked by another apartment building directly in front of what had been intended to be our dream Spanish home. This new block was not shown on the original artist's impression since it has been built by another developer. The view we had hoped to buy has gone for ever. In fact this area has turned into a concrete jungle

We had almost been caught out!

Warning: Unless you are really certain, do not buy 'off-plan'.

THE BEACH-FRONT APARTMENT

The second development we were shown was right on the beach. The apartments were very pleasant although the density of building was quite high and there was very little privacy from one terrace to another. The warning bells rang immediately: holiday rentals and probably very few long-term residents.

We discovered that this development had been started many years before and the builders had gone bust. It had lain empty for years as a concrete shell until the present developers were able to take over and start the process of completing the urbanisation. This is admirable since it means less unfinished property in the Manilva area but the warning bells started ringing when we wandered around the show apartment, which at first sight was beautiful. Good furnishings, apparently good finish to everything, but the brass door handles were turning green. This suggested a combination of dampness and sea salt and was certainly not a good omen for a lifetime free of problems in a beach-front apartment.

When we went outside the communal gardens were not terribly well looked after and the palm trees showed evidence of being a bit too close to the sea. In fact the communal gardens were really a bit of a disaster.

The entire development was very flat and featureless and was certainly not the sort of place in which we would want to spend the rest of our lives – perhaps the rest of our holidays would be more likely.

I only mention this property briefly to demonstrate the problems of beach-front living.

We rejected this property totally.

THE *FINCA* IN THE HILLS

The next day we met an estate agent who wanted to show us what he described as a wonderful little *finca* (farmhouse) in the hills behind Casares. Apparently there was a house, a large plot of land with fruit trees and olives and spectacular views. The price was a bit high but the seller might be open to offers. It sounded just what we might be looking for so off we went to see it.

We met the seller for coffee at a bar on the coast and then we set off following the seller in the estate agent's car. We climbed up towards Casares and then went beyond the town. So far, so good: the scenery was spectacular and we were climbing higher and higher into the hills. We turned off the main road – this was not a problem yet! The made-up road then turned into a dirt track with a hillside on one side and a sheer drop into the valley on the other side. The seller was driving a four wheel drive car and we were in a conventional car. There reached a point where our estate agent flashed his lights and everyone stopped. He said, 'I cannot go any further in this car' so the vendor replied, 'We are almost there, would you like to walk through the "garden" to the house?'.

The walk through the garden was amazing. We were walking through an ancient olive grove. The ground was almost ankle deep in black olives and the trees were still laden with green olives. We were not walking on grass, we were walking on wild herbs and as we walked the scent was amazing. We reached the *finca*.

It was tiny. It had three rooms. There was a kitchen/diner three metres square with very basic kitchen equipment. The living room was the same size. To reach the bedroom which was also three metres square you had to cross the terrace from the kitchen or the living room. The rooms did not connect. The vendor then said, 'Would you like to see the bath house?' We followed across the terrace and part of the garden to reach the bath house. We found a beautifully appointed bathroom with all mod cons but to get there in the middle of the night you would have to cross the garden and who knows what you might meet there in the dark?

The setting was idyllic. The house was very high up with amazing views of the surrounding mountains. On a clear day you would have a view to Gibraltar and the mountains of North Africa. There was mains electricity since the supply to Casares came across the mountain fairly close by (was it a legal spur?) and the water supply was from a private well. The actual legal boundaries of the property were a bit indistinct but that is quite normal in this part of Spain. If you walked out through the garden on your own there was absolute silence apart from the distant sound of the bells around the necks of goats in the neighbouring valley.

This was a typical example of the type of property where your heart could rule your head. It was totally impractical as it stood but there was a house there and therefore it could be possible to replace it with something more modern. The views were to die for but the approach road was one that you might die on since it was so difficult, and who would visit you for a party? Had we been 20 years younger with a lot of money to redevelop the site this could have been a marvelous purchase. The first expense would have been to have a proper road constructed to gain good access to the property.

PRACTICAL POINT

In the past the only way to build a new property in the countryside was to buy an existing property, demolish it and rebuild. This resulted in many country properties becoming very expensive because basically you had to buy the potential building land with an existing property or ruin. Recent changes to laws in Spain now mean that you can demolish the ruin but you can only rebuild to the same floor area as the original building. Therefore if you buy an old house measuring 60 square metres you can only build 60 square metres. This new law is being enforced quite strictly and makes country properties a little bit less attractive as purchases.

For us this *finca* offered no real development potential so we rejected this property with absolutely no hesitation.

THE VILLA WITH INVESTMENT POTENTIAL

The same agent took us to another house. This time it was a two-storey villa on an urbanisation. It had been converted into two apartments, each with three bedrooms. It had a wonderful garden, a beautiful swimming pool and views down to the sea. The English owners wanted to move further along the coast, which was why they were selling (or so they said). The ground floor apartment was let for holidays and the owners stated that the rental income was very good and was their only source of income. There was also a lot of repeat business.

So far so good. It was expensive but almost within our price range. We would be buying a home and an investment all in one. This property was very tempting. However when we thought about it more carefully we did not really like the idea of the investment property being the ground floor of our own home. We would have to share the swimming pool and we might not even like the tenants.

How lucky we were.

There was open land in front of the property and a field to the side of it. Since we considered buying the property this land has been built on. There is now a new development of small villas which completely block the view to the sea. I doubt if there will be so much repeat business for rentals in the future. The real question that remains is: did the vendors know about the planned development and was that why they were selling? Did they hope that the purchaser would not discover that there was a development planned? The field to the side of the house which apparently had been empty for years is now the site of a development of apartments which will block the view from this house towards Estepona Bay.

Another rejection!

THE VILLAGE HOUSE

The next property we viewed as a potential purchase was described as a village house with potential to create a large family home. This could be just what we were looking for: a home in a real Spanish town with lots of atmosphere. So off we went to see it.

The climb up to the property was quite spectacular but the house had a private driveway leading up to a parking area which was on level ground. We went inside to discover a property which probably had great potential but not for us. The house was actually two houses which had been knocked into one and when I say knocked into one, I mean just that. If there was a wall the owners had demolished it. There were eight rooms including three bathrooms and two kitchens. One room was very proudly shown to us as an alternative sitting room, but when we pulled the curtains at the far end of the room we found an up and over door. It was actually the garage! Because the two houses were not exactly on the same level there were terraces everywhere. The garden to the back sloped so steeply that you could not even have walked down the garden, never mind cultivate it. Potential it had, but not for us. There would be too much work involved in fixing the botched up knocking together of two houses.

Another rejection!

THE COUNTRY PROPERTY

Our estate agent contacted us one day and said she had a property for sale out in the country – the *campo*. We agreed to see it; after all, it might be just the house we were looking for. Off we went. The property was about 10 miles inland but it was at the end of a pot-holed dirt track. No problem in daylight since you could see the pot holes but driving back after dark could have been a nightmare and it would certainly not have been good for the suspension of any car apart from a very rugged 4x4. In addition, I doubt if many friends would have wanted to visit us in the evening and have to face the return journey in the dark.

The house was in the middle of nowhere with views out over the countryside. There were fields with horses grazing. There were views of the distant hills and mountains. It was amazingly quiet with only the sound of birdsong to break the silence. There were some problems which we could anticipate. It would probably be incredibly hot in the summer months since it was in a valley surrounded by hills. Visiting the supermarket would be a major exercise. There were no immediate neighbours so what would happen if you had an emergency and needed help? Would security be a problem? It would be potentially very dark at night and very remote.

The house itself was beautiful. It was modern and built U-shape around a very nice swimming pool courtyard. There was a modern double garage at the end of a long drive and a large well-stocked garden. Had it been closer to civilisation it would have been our dream home, but would also have been outside our price range.

Once more, a rejection.

THE VILLA WITH A VIEW

We had not given up on the idea of living in a house rather than in an apartment and when we saw a small villa advertised within our price range in an urbanisation close to where we were now living (we had moved to Spain and were now looking for a second property) we just had to see it. We checked it out from the outside first and were bowled over by the potential views. It was right

on the edge of a ridge on very high ground with
spectacular views over the entire bay of Estepona.
Nothing could possibly be built in front of this property
since the hillside was too steep. That was an immediate
plus. There were steps down to the house from the road
and a very large terrace on this level which faced south
and west. It looked as if the view from the actual garden
would be amazing. It seemed ideal and we wanted to see
inside so a viewing was arranged for the next day.

First viewing

Two very excited people met the agent outside the villa
the next morning. The door was unlocked and at first
sight the house was wonderful. Admittedly, it was to be
sold furnished and we hated the furniture. We hated the
colour schemes but that would be easy to fix. The kitchen
needed to be modernised – not really a problem. A few
internal walls needed to be moved around to improve the
layout of the house, but everything was possible. The
garden was beautiful. Established fruit trees and palms.
Terraced paths and garden down to a paved terrace on
the edge of the ridge and the views! At this stage we were
really excited about this house. The heart was beginning
to take over!

Second viewing

We thought about it very carefully and decided that this
could probably be the house for us, so we arranged to see
it for a second time. On the second occasion we visited
this house with friends who were also keen to see it.

While the agent showed our friends around we wandered through the house on our own. Then the problems started to show up and there were quite a few. The storm drain from the road went through a channel just underneath the front terrace. This could potentially be a problem in very heavy rain, particularly if the channel became blocked with plant debris. The terrace could flood.

Then we noticed that there was a gap of about two millimetres under the front door. If the terrace flooded the house could flood, but why was the gap there in the first place? The ground floor apart from the state of decoration was not too much of a problem but when we looked carefully at the top floor bedroom we realised that it had been a roof terrace which had been enclosed – and I mean enclosed. The windows did not open at all. There was a door to a smaller roof terrace but this had no parapet. This room and terrace needed major work to make it both livable and safe.

Finally we had a really good look at the garden and noticed that every major plant had stones around it in the direction of the hillside. Obviously when it rains (and in the Costa del Sol it can rain really hard) there must be a real danger of soil erosion. We then went down to the final paved terrace on the edge of the ridge and noticed that the parapet of the terrace had cracks in it, the paving stones of the terrace were cracked at the edge and there was a gap between the paving and the parapet.

We then realised why we could afford this house. It was sliding off the edge of the ridge, or at least the garden was. This discovery explained the gap under the front door. The ground was dropping.

Since we decided not to buy this property the hillside in front of the house which looked too steep to build on has been blasted with dynamite and a block of flats is currently under construction.

PRACTICAL POINT

I use these examples of our househunting experiences to reinforce the danger of making any decision based on short inspection trips and quick decisions made in the company of a very persuasive estate agent. We saw many of these properties after we were actually living in Spain. We were able to go back and inspect them more carefully and let the mind overrule the heart. Had we seen some of them on one of our earlier trips when we were first looking we might have been inclined to make an offer and buy. We would have been seeing them once and going back to England the next day with only a memory of what we had seen. We could have been buying trouble.

WHAT DID WE BUY AND WHY DID WE BUY IT?

On our very first viewing trip to Spain you will remember that we were advised by one agent either to rent first or to buy an inexpensive property which would resell easily when we found the property we really wanted to live in. As you will have gathered, we did not take this advice and started the process described above when we put down a deposit to buy off-plan. We only discovered the problems when we came back to Spain two months later to sign the deed of sale and that was when we pulled out of that first purchase. On that trip were two friends who wanted to buy an apartment and we went with them to view properties. There was one apartment they viewed which we loved. It was in an established development. It had views over magnificent sub-tropical gardens and a huge lagoon-style swimming pool. Beyond this was a golf course and then a hillside which, although developed, was far enough away not to obstruct the view.

Our friends rejected this apartment because the terrace did not face south. It faced east and only had the sun in the morning. We liked this apartment very much and regretted that we had not seen it before we entered into negotiations to buy the off-plan apartment described above. That very evening we were scheduled to visit our lawyer to sign the deed of sale on the off-plan apartment.

Following the events of the visit to the lawyer when we cancelled the purchase and remembering the advice we had been given that the Spanish only buy east- or even north-facing, we jumped in the next morning and made an offer. It was accepted. Within two months we were the owners of a two bedroom apartment on the Costa del Sol.

This first apartment was almost perfect. Nothing could ever change the views from the terrace. It was affordable and if we ever wanted to get rid of it it should sell relatively easily. It would also be a very good rental apartment should we decide in the long term to keep it as an investment.

This is the apartment to which we finally moved when we left the UK.

Our first Spanish apartment

We were very happy in this apartment. It had almost everything we wished for. The marble floors were cool in the summer. The east-facing orientation kept the apartment very cool. We had views. We were on the edge of the countryside but only one kilometre from the sea on high ground. Evenings and mornings were blissfully quiet. We even went out to buy a book on birds since there were so many interesting birds flying around which we could not identify.

However, we continued the process of looking for the property which would be our home long term. I have recounted some of our experiences, but every time we went out to look we returned home to our new apartment and thought we really cannot do much better than this. There is virtually nothing in our price range that compares with what we already have. This was the time when we really started to take note of the advice to 'buy what you need, not what you want'.

Our second apartment

A few months into our Spanish adventure, our estate agent friend rang us up to say that she had just taken instructions on another apartment in the same development, only this time it was a three bedroom duplex (two floors) with three terraces. It was twice the size of our first apartment and it had the same orientation to the east. Were we interested?

The next morning we went to view. It was exactly what we wanted. It had space. It was decorated exactly to our taste and was also to be sold furnished and we liked the furnishings. The terraces were three-quarters the size of our London townhouse garden – they would become an outdoor room. Within 30 minutes we had made our decision. For once heart and mind were in unison and we made an offer which was accepted. Two months later we moved in and since the price was well within our budget we were able to retain the first apartment as an investment for holiday rentals.

This experience only goes to show what I have tried to say throughout this chapter. The right property does exist for everyone but it is easier to find if you are on the spot when it becomes available and can move fast.

BUYING OFF-PLAN

Buying off-plan is a common way to buy new property in Spain. There can be positives with this route of buying,

particularly if you are buying as an investment and you
have little intention of actually living in the property
when it is finished. *You may even want to become a
property speculator and I would be the first to say that
there is nothing wrong with that.* Everyone is entitled to
make a living. Speculators often sell unfinished buildings
during the period that the building work is progressing. If
the speculator has bought before building has even
started and all that had been bought was an artist's
impression the prices can appear to be very low at this
stage in the process. When the property is half completed
it can often be sold on at a higher price and that is before
the speculator has even paid the full price of the new
property. There are even adverts in the quality English
Sunday newspapers telling potential speculators how they
can profit from buying property in the Spanish market
without ever paying the full price for the property. This is
fine if you are in business to make money from buying
and selling property.

However, if, like us, you are looking for your dream
home, it is a different matter. When you make your
decision to buy off-plan you will be essentially buying an
artist's impression and a drawing of the floor plan of your
future apartment or house. Would you consider paying
considerably more than £100,000 for a painting? This is
what you are in effect doing. In the process you are also
indirectly funding the building work as the building
progresses and proving to the bank which funds the
developer that the properties are actually selling. The

banks funding the development will therefore leave the funding in place to allow for completion. Any money you pay to the developer as a deposit and as staged payments should, by law, be held in a separate bank account and you should ask your Spanish lawyer to check this point.

In addition, when buying off-plan, you do not know whether or not the building will have defects – and many new buildings do. The other potential problem is that of the actual delivery date of the property. In Spain most new properties are delivered late and sometimes very late – even up to a year behind schedule. This is despite the fact that Spanish law states that a purchase contract must specify a delivery date. You can, of course, negotiate a late delivery penalty clause whereby the developer will pay you an agreed sum for every day that building work exceeds the agreed date. However, many sellers will simply ignore this or offer you your money back as a gesture of goodwill.

What happens if delivery is late?

By this stage your money will have helped indirectly to fund the building programme and what you now want is the property not your money back. The developers may actually be only too happy to offer you a refund since they know that the property is now worth more than it was when you first entered into the off-plan agreement so if you pull out they can sell it at a higher price. The developer will often get around the problem of late delivery by passing the buck to the local town hall. Before anyone can move in the new property must have a First Occupation License, *la licencia de primera ocupacion.* Currently there are properties under construction near to us where this license will not be granted by the town hall until the developers return the access roads to the condition they were in before building started, since the builders have wreaked havoc on the roads, pavements and drains. Even if these apartment blocks are finished and ready for occupation not one single person can move in. Should you find yourself in such a situation the developer may blame the local town hall rather than telling you that it is because of their actions that the local town hall has refused the license.

Illegal occupation

There have also been occasions when new buyers have moved unofficially (and illegally!) into the new property before this license has been granted. Some of these new residents have continued to use the developers' electricity and water supply for as long as a year until all the paperwork has been completed. The developers often encourage this action.

Your money

You must also ensure that the money you pay up-front is in fact paid into a separate bank account covered by an insurance policy. There have been occasions in the past when people have bought off-plan and the builder has gone bankrupt, taking clients' money with him. Should

the builder go bankrupt you are entitled to a refund of all
the money you have paid plus interest.

Disadvantages of off-plan purchase

Having had one unfortunate experience with an aborted
off-plan purchase I personally would never consider
buying in this way (remember our first case history).
There are other disadvantages to off-plan purchasing.
Among these are the fact that the communal gardens in
an urbanisation will take years to be at their best. There
may be no swimming pool when you first move into your
dream property. The community charge is not actually set
until a Board of Management has been appointed so you
have no way of knowing what your overheads might be.
You cannot talk to neighbours who already live in the
development to ask if there are problems with noise
transmission between floors or through the walls. You
have no way of knowing whether the development will be
primarily residential or primarily holiday homes or a
mixture of both. If you are moving into a large
development, unless you are buying in the final phase you
may end up living on a building site for several years until
the development is completed.

When you inspect the prospective property the developer
must show you the plans of the buildings and the gardens
together with a detailed specification of the building
materials to be used. All this should be in your contract
and if the developer does not match the contract details
the law is on your side – or should be.

A real-life off-plan case history

Where we live is well established and our apartments were built 22 years ago. They are well built and there has been no major structural problem.

There is land close to us on the top of the next hill which, when we moved to Spain, was undeveloped and was actually shown on the plan of the urbanisation as 'green land' with no plans to build. This is what a Spanish lawyer would have found on the plans! There are now five four-storey apartment blocks on the top of this hill. Building started before planning permission was granted but it has now been given retrospectively. The sales office at the entrance to this urbanisation has a wonderful scale model of the development, which allowed potential buyers to buy off-plan and select those apartments which would have the best views of the bay. We watched as potential buyers came to look at the building site and checked out where their apartment would be. Potential buyers were buying their dream property on the Costa del Sol!

Then the same company decided to develop a very small piece of land nearby which had planning permission for four villas to be built. Are they building four villas? No, they are building 16 three-storey townhouses which will effectively block the view of the bay which the buyers of the off-plan apartments think they have. The sales literature for the townhouses shows 16 houses in a wonderful artist's impression of a site in the middle of the countryside with unobstructed views to the hills and to the mountains and this will be distributed at property shows in the UK. At these shows organised by some of the largest sellers of property in Spain, unsuspecting punters might be persuaded to pay a 10 per cent deposit against one of these wonderful houses. Nowhere on the artist's impression is a picture of the five apartment blocks, which are almost complete!

But the two developments are being built by the same company!

By law all information contained in advertising materials must be correct. If a pool is shown on the plan but does not materialise you have redress in law.

You must ensure that the developer is responsible for a tax called the *plus valia*, a municipal tax payable on the increased value of the property and the land after completion – you should not be liable for this. It is the developer who is making the profit so he should pay the taxes, not you.

If the developer tries to charge you a cancellation fee for a mortgage which you do not want or need and have not agreed to he is out of line and you can refuse to pay.

When you have signed the contract and agreed to make staged payments these must be paid by the date stipulated otherwise the vendor has the right to terminate the contract and you could lose all the money you have already paid. The property will then be re-sold to another purchaser – probably at a higher price.

Should you be considering an off-plan purchase then *please* take note of all the above points. Personally I think it is a very foolish way to buy a property. Resale properties make much more sense to my mind since you can actually see what you are buying and talk to neighbours. You can also see if there have been any

PRACTICAL POINT

Any off-plan purchase demands the services of your own, personally appointed Spanish lawyer. Do *not* use the developer's lawyer, whose first loyalty must be to the developer.

Remember at all times it is YOUR money. Think carefully before you hand it over!

problems with the quality of construction over the years that your new purchase has existed. Therefore you are less likely to make a terrible mistake.

5

Legal Matters

When you finally decide to buy a property in Spain, it is
absolutely vital that you retain the services of an
independent Spanish lawyer experienced in Spanish
property law who is retained by you and you alone. The
amount of money you may commit to a property
purchase is considerable and it is vital that absolutely
nothing is left to chance. Never sign any document or pay
any money without first consulting your lawyer. Many
British purchasers do not obtain independent legal advice
and many have lived to regret it. Some only consult a

lawyer when problems arise, but this might be too late. There is no excuse for not retaining the services of an independent lawyer since legal costs in Spain are much lower than the equivalent costs in the UK.

PRACTICAL POINT

It is not advisable to trust the advice given to you by someone who has a vested interest in the prospective sale such as the developer or the estate agent. A good maxim is trust no one!

Without the services of a good Spanish lawyer when we first started the process of buying an apartment off-plan we would have had far more difficulty getting out of the contract and having our deposit returned.

Despite the fact that both the UK and Spain are in the European Union there are major legal differences between EU countries and you must be aware of this. Although this book deals primarily with our experiences, I think it worthwhile to describe the various legal pitfalls in which you could be ensnared.

SHOULD YOU HAVE THE PROPERTY SURVEYED?

Starting from the point at which you find your dream property, the first thing to do is to decide whether or not you want to have it subjected to a full structural survey.

For relatively new properties this may not be necessary so long as the property has been built by a reputable builder. Any properties over 10 years old will no longer be covered by a builder's warranty and should be examined carefully. There are many examples of sub-standard buildings constructed in the 1960s and 1970s when the boom period for building first arrived in the Costa del Sol.

New property?

I have to say that many new 'luxury' properties (some close to where we live now) have also been built in a similar sub-standard fashion. We have seen the concrete foundations for the ground floor laid directly onto the surface of the land without any form of damp-proof membrane being laid. We have seen the plastic sewer pipes being laid in a trench with no hardcore or concrete surrounding them. Does this sound like a good foundation for a future free of problems?

Is the property legal?

If your dream property is a villa or a *finca* (farmhouse) standing on its own land you need to check whether all the land you have been told belongs to the house actually does. Is the land on the *escritura* (title deeds). You also need to check that the house actually exists in law. Is the house on the *escritura*? There have been many examples of *escrituras* which list the land but have no listing of the house which is built on that land. If the property is on the edge of a hillside you need your surveyor to check that

the land is stable. The last thing you want to see is your
dream falling down the side of a hill. Remember our
experience with the little villa with the views!

Rural property?

If the property is rural, do all the services work well? We
saw one house which had electricity generated locally but
two of the three generators needed to be replaced. What
is the condition of the septic tank if the house depends on
this for waste disposal? If the property depends on well
water, what is the condition of the well? We know many
people here who depend on a natural (and I have to say
free!) water supply for their daily needs and they have no
problems whatsoever, but the well needs to be deep
enough to reach the richest supply of fresh water and the
pump which brings that water to the surface needs to be
powerful enough to do the job properly. All these things
can only be checked by a properly qualified surveyor.

If the house is in a rural area and you are viewing in the
hotter months of the year, what will it be like when it
rains? When it rains on the Costa del Sol, it rains heavily.
Flash floods are not uncommon in rural areas and you
should check that the property is nowhere near a dried-up
river bed. Continuing on the subject of the problems of
moisture, many older properties in Spain do not have
adequate damp-courses. This may not be apparent in the
height of the Andalucian summer when everything is
tinder dry, but what is the property like after a
particularly heavy fall of rain? If the house of your

dreams is at the end of a dirt track, is this dirt track accessible after very heavy rain? The estate agent may have taken you there on a perfectly dry summer day when the only problem is dust. What happens when there is mud?

Should you decide to buy an old village house as a restoration project you should have a proper survey carried out to check the real condition of the building. If you fall in love with an old house which has already been restored you should ask to see the invoices for the restoration work so that you can check exactly what has been done.

Once more the important thing to remember is not to let your heart rule your head. The most idyllic property could turn into a nightmare if you experience problems in the future.

This subject is dealt with in far more detail in *Buying a Home in Spain* by David Hampshire (Survival Books). I recommend that anyone buying a home in Spain should read this book thoroughly from cover to cover. It was our bible during our moving period.

THE CONVEYANCE

This is the legal term for processing all the necessary paperwork involved in buying and selling a property and transferring the title deeds from one owner to another.

Unlike in the UK, in Spain some aspects of the
conveyance can only be done by a representative of the
Spanish government, the notary (*notario*) whose job it is

PRACTICAL POINTS

Your *own personally appointed* lawyer needs to
check the following points:

◆ Does the property actually belong to the person
who is selling it and does the vendor have the
right to sell? If the property has been left to a
family as a legacy, every member of the family
has to agree to the sale. If the property has no
escritura, be very wary. It might have been on the
site for years but if it does not 'exist' legally you
could find what you consider to be your land
being repossessed by the local council, especially
if redevelopment is planned.

◆ What is the value of the property and the land
and what price does the vendor want to put on
the *escritura*? If there is ever any dispute in the
future and the land is wanted for redevelopment
the sum you will be offered will be based on the
value declared in the *escritura*. There are many
vendors who want to put as little as possible on
the *escritura* because it reduces the amount of tax
they have to pay, but be very wary of this
practice! It is actually illegal to underdeclare the
value of the property, although many people do.

◆ Are there tenants in the property and if so, will they move out to allow you to move in?

◆ What other building works are planned for the area? Remember our experience with the apartment we almost bought which now has another block in front of it obscuring part of the view, and the villa with the self-contained rental apartment on the ground floor. Are there any plans for new roads or railways? All these things can be checked by your lawyer.

◆ Does the *escritura* list the land and the property and is it accurate? If there is a lot of land with the property, is it fenced or carefully marked out in some way?

◆ Have all the bills been paid? In Spain bills accompany the property so if the mortgage has not been paid, you will inherit the mortgage. This is called the law of subrogation. Have the gas, electricity and telephone bills been paid? Have the local authority rates been paid? If you are buying in an urbanisation, have the community charges been paid? Remember, you could inherit these debts. Some UK buyers have been very badly affected by such charges because they thought they did not need a lawyer.

to ensure that all the state taxes due are paid on completion of the sale and that all outstanding bills have been paid to their satisfaction. You will still need to employ your own independent lawyer. A good, bilingual lawyer is important since they will need to take you through the *escritura*, which will be written in Spanish.

Many developers will claim to carry out all these checks for you, but you should still employ an independent lawyer to act for you. The developer simply wants to sell. He is looking after his interests. Only **you** can look after your own interests.

THE PURCHASE CONTRACT

Whenever anyone buys a property in Spain the first step is usually the signing of a private contract of sale. At this stage it is common to pay a 10 per cent deposit and agree a time span for the completion of the sale or the timetable for the payment of staged payments if you are buying off-plan. You need to remember that this deposit is officially non-returnable should you decide not to proceed but also that should the vendor decide not to proceed they will have to return to you 20 per cent of the agreed price.

Buying furnished

There is one further feature of buying property in Spain which must be mentioned. It is very common for villas, townhouses and apartments to be sold fully furnished.

Owners moving to a new home leave everything in the property they are selling – and I mean everything. The second property we bought even included the food in the kitchen cupboards and the contents of the drinks cabinet. When a property is being sold in this way it is important that an inventory is drawn up listing all the items which are to be left. It could be very tempting to buy a property which is being sold fully furnished if you like the furnishings. Think how unhappy you would be if you finally took possession and found that the beautiful furniture you thought you were buying with the property had been replaced by tacky furniture which you just have to throw out.

COMPLETION

This is the special day when you actually take possession of your new property in Spain. It will usually be two to three months after you signed the original contract of sale but it could be earlier if you want a quick purchase. Completion must be carried out in the presence of the notary public, although you can appoint someone with the power of attorney to represent you. It is at this stage that the money changes hands and the title deed, the *escritura*, is transferred. If you are buying a furnished property you should visit it just before the visit to the notary to ensure that all the fixtures and fittings listed on the inventory are still there. Have the kitchen fittings been replaced by second-hand items which do not match the quality of what you agreed to purchase? If this is the

case the completion can be delayed until everything is
agreed to your satisfaction, but if you sign, the deed is
done and you have no way of turning back the clock.

After the sale has been completed you need to ensure
that the property is registered in your name at the
property registry office. This is one further reason for
employing a Spanish lawyer to act for you. If the property
is not registered in your name any outstanding charges
can still be registered against the property without you
being contacted.

6

The Actual Removal

We had found the property we wanted to live in (our first Spanish apartment). We were now making progress. We were buying furnished but we planned to move most of the existing furniture into store and move our furniture into the apartment. Later, when we found another property, we would use the furniture in storage to furnish our letting apartment. It all seemed so simple.

It was not! The first step we had to take was to really look very carefully at all the possessions we had in the

UK. Did we need them? Did we use them? Did we even like them? Would they fit into a Spanish apartment? We had lived in the same house for 16 years so you can imagine how much we had accumulated in that time. We had a really good look at our possessions and had a massive clear-out. We had to bear in mind that everything we took to Spain would cost money to transport there so we were ruthless. This turned out to be a wonderful opportunity to take stock of all our possessions.

NEAR-DISASTER

Then we made our first mistake. We obtained estimates from mainstream removal companies who were prepared to transport personal belongings to Spain. We also had estimates from smaller companies who advertise in the English language newspapers in Spain. Needless to say, they were cheaper, so we decided to give our business to one of these companies. We accepted a verbal estimate which was then backed up by a handwritten estimate.

We had also bought a left-hand-drive vehicle which we wanted to take to our new home. The removers offered to transport it on a trailer for us, which seemed like a very good idea. The cost seemed reasonable and it would save us the nightmare drive across France and Spain with the dog in the back of the car. We could fly to Spain with the dog and a few days later our furniture and our car would arrive to complete the removal process. The remover we had selected would arrange for the furniture we wished to put into store to be picked up from the apartment and taken to a suitable storage place. The date for the removal was agreed.

Everything appeared to be totally in order and we even recommended this removal company to two other couples who were in the process of moving to Spain.

Our first surprise came when the removers arrived two days before the agreed date. It was a Monday morning and we were sitting quite happily at the dining room table reading the paper when the doorbell rang.

'We've come to move you, Guv'.

Panic set in. We were totally unprepared at that time for removers to turn up. However, they said that they just wanted to start packing so that the removal would take place properly on the Wednesday of that week. Warning bells should have rung when I saw the removal van – an anonymous white van, not very new and with absolutely no markings of any kind on the side – but it was too late to start again, we had to be prepared to trust this company.

In they came and they started to pack our belongings. They did work relatively quickly and when we finally unpacked at the other end there were only two minor breakages. They also packed very thoroughly. When we finally unpacked in Spain we found a copy of the *Sunday*

Times which had been lying on the dining room table. They also packed china which had not been intended for Spain – it was destined for the rubbish bin but we were using it until the very last moment. When the packers asked if there was any chance of a cup of coffee or tea, we discovered that tea, coffee and sugar had all been packed and we did not have any clue as to which box they were in.

By the end of the first day of packing we were left with our TV, two chairs and a bed to sleep on. The car had also been used as a container for some of our belongings with clothes used to provide protection for fragile items. This would prove to be a bit of a problem later.

By the end of the second day we were able to leave our London house for the last time. We then had to pay for the removal in advance, and because we were taking house plants with us which required the full height of the back of the van we were asked to pay considerably more than the original quotation. We were now occupying the entire loadspace of the van and there was no possibility of our belongings being classed as a part load. We paid up. We also paid for insurance – another additional cost. The price was now twice the level of the original estimate.

In retrospect the other very silly thing we did was not to compile an inventory of what was being transported either from the UK or from the Spanish apartment into storage. We were just too trusting.

As we set off in the taxi to the airport we took a look at the anonymous white van parked outside our home of 16 years which contained all our worldly possessions, fully expecting to see it again within a few days. By this time the car had been driven off to be put on a trailer, which would be attached to another delivery van destined for Spain.

Last night in the UK

Our last night in the UK was horrendous. We were flying from Luton to Gibraltar early the next morning so we decided that it would probably be better to stay overnight at an airport hotel in order to avoid a ridiculously early start. We booked into a well-known hotel chain and I have to say that it did seem very cheap. What they did not tell us when we booked was the fact that the hotel was at the end of the runway and Luton airport has night flights all night. There was no way that we could even consider sleeping with the windows open. I have to say it was not the most comfortable night that we have spent in a hotel.

The Spanish adventure begins

The next morning our Spanish adventure began in earnest. It was the first time that we had ever flown on a one-way ticket and that was a bit scary in retrospect. Turning back would now be more difficult. Our belongings were following (we hoped) and our friends were waiting to meet us in Gibraltar. Just over two hours after leaving Luton we stepped off the plane onto the tarmac in Gibraltar. Our new life was about to begin.

We drove to our apartment and moved into our new home. Although we were still living with the furniture we had inherited, the place would truly be home in a few days. We had been told that the furniture would take about a week to arrive and as the days of that first week progressed we began to get more and more excited.

One week later there was absolutely no sign of the arrival of our furniture and possessions. We rang the UK number for the removal company – no answer. Not even an answering machine. We tried ringing the mobile number we had been given for the driver. It was not switched on. Eventually we were able to speak to the driver only to discover that the van was still in northern Spain. It would be another two or three days before it reached us. All we could do was to wait and try to be patient and philosophical. We now realised that we had made a mistake.

Finally the van arrived, ten days after leaving London. It was the hottest day of the year and they started to unpack our belongings. Some of the house plants had rotted a bit in the heat of the back of the van (although most did recover eventually). The inherited furniture which we wanted to put into storage was carried out of the apartment and loaded into another smaller van to be taken to a store in Estepona. We were not given a receipt. We were not given an inventory. We were not given a destination address. We were totally trusting. This was the last we ever saw of this furniture.

Our furniture had arrived but our car had not, and it contained most of our changes of clothing. We finally managed to get through to the proprietor of the removal company on his mobile and the conversation went as follows:

'Where are you and where is our car?'

'Don't worry, I am just crossing the border and that is why you could not get hold of me.'

'Do you mean the French/Spanish border?'

'Oh no, the border between Croatia and Austria! When I get back to the UK I will get your car out to you.'

We were dumbfounded. This was beginning to be a bit of a farce. Was this really happening?

A week later the car was driven up to the front door of the apartment but not by the proprietor of the company. I do not think he dared face us. He did send us a cheque to pay for the additional car hire we had incurred but when I tried to claim on the insurance for some minor breakages we received absolutely no compensation. The company to which we had entrusted our belongings was quite simply bankrupt. They did not exist any more.

The insurance payment was bogus!

A NIGHTMARE EXPERIENCE

Our experiences were bad enough but the experiences of some friends to whom we had recommended this company were just as bizarre. They were mother, father and three children moving to Spain to start a new life. They were moving from London to Mijas lock, stock and barrel. The removers arrived and started packing. Their entire worldly possessions were loaded into the anonymous white van. Again, there was no inventory. Off the van went and the family flew to Spain to start their new life fully expecting their belongings to arrive at their Spanish villa in a few days. They did not!

They were unlucky enough to be moving a couple of weeks after our removal and by this time this unfortunate cowboy company had gone bankrupt. The main difference between their story and ours was that they had not paid up front. They could not make contact by telephone – landline or mobile. At worst they got no response, at best they got the answering machine. Their belongings were somewhere between London and the Costa del Sol on a van which was being driven by individuals who were owed money by their employers and who were not prepared to deliver the furniture until they were paid for their work. Our friends finally managed to speak to someone on the telephone and the result was like something from a film.

The van drivers were not prepared to deliver the goods until they had been paid. The company did not have the

money to pay them so the van drivers were not prepared
to say where they were in Spain. The poor owners of the
contents of the van began to despair that they would ever
see the contents of their house again. Basically the drivers
of the van had stolen their possessions and would
probably sell them to recover some of the wages owed to
them by their bankrupt employers. Finally a compromise
was reached and a plan was suggested. A price was
agreed for the delivery of the belongings which would be
paid to the van drivers. The van would drive to the
bottom of the road where our friends lived and one of our
friends would go to meet them there and pay the agreed
sum in cash. Only when this had been done would the van
drive up the hill to our friends' villa and deliver their
belongings.

Our friends agreed to this plan, but did not go to the
various meeting places alone or stay in the property
alone. They were genuinely very scared by all this cloak
and dagger stuff. The story does, however, have a happy
ending. They paid the money in a brown paper envelope.
Their furniture (including father's wide screen television
and digibox for the football) was delivered and they are
now blissfully happy living in the sun of the Costa del Sol
with the horrors of the removal in the past.

(Footnote to the experience: nine months later we were
contacted by a storage company in Estepona who
informed us that they believed they had some of our
possessions in storage. By this time we had bought our

PRACTICAL POINT

The moral of the stories recounted in the previous pages is simple. Removals can be expensive. Do not cut corners on this most important aspect of the start of your new life. Go to an established company with a reputation to maintain and avoid the cowboys. Happily we and our friends had a happy outcome to the nightmares of a removal but it could so easily have been very different.

second apartment which had been purchased fully furnished. We did not need what had been taken from the first apartment so we told them to sell it. We had not signed any contract or been told where our belongings were so as far as we were concerned we had lost them.)

7

Settling In

We had made it. Ten months after taking the momentous decision to change our lifestyle we finally stepped off the plane into the Spanish sun.

Had we made the right decision? We certainly hoped so. We had sold up totally in Britain and going back would be difficult. We would certainly not be able to afford to return to the London area, even if we wanted to.

How long would it take for us to feel totally at home in

our new environment? There was a little nagging doubt that we would never feel at home. After all, we were now in another country with different attitudes and lifestyle.

We were going to be in a semi-retired situation. Would we be bored? We did not enjoy some of the things that retirees to the Costa del Sol usually do, like playing golf or bridge. Would the days seem too long? How would we occupy our time?

How long would it take to come to terms with the fact that Spain was now our home? We were not in Spain for a holiday. We were here for good!

FIRST IMPRESSIONS

The first few weeks were strange and we definitely felt as if we were on holiday. There was also the fact that our own furniture was still in transit so we were essentially living in what had been someone's holiday home. This was added to by the fact that we moved from the UK on the 1st August so we had arrived in our new home at the height of the tourist season. The roads were very busy since the new coast road was still under construction. The restaurants were busy, the bars were busy and there was that buzz which you always experience in an area where people have come to escape from their everyday life.

Our new apartment was in a complex (an urbanisation, as we described earlier), but we very quickly realised that this should not really be a problem. We had a wonderful swimming pool but there were no restaurants, bars, tennis courts, football pitches or anything like that around the complex. There were people on holiday in August but apart from the sound of children enjoying themselves in the pool during the day (some children do scream a bit) the mornings and evenings were generally blissfully quiet. Overnight it was even more quiet and when we woke up at three in the morning it was almost as if we had died. There was just no sound at all.

This was a major change from what we had been accustomed to in London. We had lived for 16 years under a take-off flight path from Heathrow airport and suddenly there was no aircraft noise. In fact we hardly ever see an aircraft and when we do it is high in the sky and all we see are the vapour trails. The only thing we see flying now are birds. Since we are not on a main road there is no passing traffic and we are far enough away from the coast road to escape the noise of through traffic.

THE PRACTICAL SIDE OF THINGS

Whenever you move house there are always practical things to be attended to such as gas, electricity, telephones, local taxes, insurance and everything else which is an everyday part of modern life. To smooth your way through all this in Spain it can be helpful if you have a local contact who speaks fluent Spanish since not all the service providers speak fluent English (and, of course, why should they?).

GAS

Should you buy a property with gas as part of the services it really is very easy to get organised. There is no mains gas in the south of Spain so you will be dependent on bottled gas. If you buy a resale property it is likely that you will inherit a couple of gas cylinders on which the legal deposit has already been made. If this is the case you either need to keep your eyes open for the gas delivery service which will exchange an empty cylinder for a newly filled one at very minimal cost or you need to find out where the nearest depot is and take the cylinder along yourself to exchange it. In our case we are lucky since there is a local delivery service, although at first we thought it was an ice cream seller because of the bells he was ringing. If there is no regular local delivery a simple phone call to the nearest gas depot will result in a cylinder being delivered straight to your door and if you are going to be out you can leave the empty cylinder outside the door with the payment underneath. I have to say that gas is by far the cheapest way to cook and heat water.

If you have moved to a new property which has gas water heating or cooking you will need to go along to your local gas supplier and sign a contract for the gas bottles. Once the contract has been signed you will then be entitled to exchange gas bottles in perpetuity. I wouldn't encourage anyone to break the law but you can get the same result if you go to the local market and buy a couple of empty gas bottles. You can then exchange them for filled bottles at any gas depot. The depot actually encourages people to do this since it saves the bureaucracy of opening a new account.

ELECTRICITY

Electricity was a bit more of a problem since the people at the electricity company were not bilingual and in order to have the electricity service transferred to our name we needed to have a new meter fitted. This was where our Spanish-speaking estate agent was very useful and it was accomplished very easily and with no delays.

One minor chore you will encounter when you move to Spain is to change the plugs on all the English electrical equipment you have brought to Spain for the Spanish variety. It is easier to do this rather than having to use adapters for your English plugs. Another minor inconvenience is that Spanish light fittings have screw-in bulbs and you need to ensure that you have a constant supply of bayonet fit bulbs for any English lamps you have transported to Spain. These are one of the things we often ask visitors to bring when they come to stay.

Power cuts are a fact of life in many parts of Spain. They can last for a few minutes or several hours. Happily the

latter scenario is not that common. They can be a bit
inconvenient because in many properties water may be
delivered to your home by electric pump so a power cut
also means no water supply.

You can also be caught out if you do not understand
Spanish electrical systems fully. Most new buildings have
circuit breakers which can trip if there is a power surge.
The first time this happened we thought we were
suffering from a power cut. We only discovered it was the
trip switch after 20 minutes when we suddenly realised
that all our neighbours appeared to have power. Now the
first thing we check when we have no electricity is the trip
switch.

TELEPHONES

Telephones are not a problem since the telecommuni-
cations industry is multinational and you will always find
someone at the end of the phone who speaks English. In
fact in Spain when you ring the telephone company
you are invited to press the appropriate button for an
English-speaking customer service assistant. If you buy a
resale property with a phone already installed it is not
difficult to have the account transferred. On both
occasions when we asked for this to be done we were told
it might take up to a week. On both occasions it was done
within a day. We have, however, heard of people who
have had quite long delays in having a new telephone line
installed. There are also a number of companies in Spain

who offer reduced rate calls both locally and internationally by registering and dialing a special code before the number you want to call. These companies have saved us a fortune, particularly as many of our calls are international back to friends in the UK.

If you need to have a new line installed, it could be a good idea to have the back up of a mobile telephone until the land line is in place. Mobiles in Spain are much less of a problem than they are in Britain. If you move to Spain with a functioning UK mobile it is possible to change the chip at minimal cost and switch to a prepay service for which you can purchase more airtime at the local supermarket, garage or even the ATM machine. You don't have to purchase a new telephone. In addition, when we bought a new chip for our phone it automatically brought up the instructions in English. Should you decide to split your time between the UK and Spain you could buy a Spanish phone chip for the times you are in Spain and use the same handset in both countries.

One problem is that UK land telephones do not work in Spain. Quite apart from the fact that you need an adapter for the plug since the Spanish telephone system uses plugs similar to those in the USA there appears to be a problem with the frequency and a UK phone does not ring in Spain. You can use an adapter and make calls but you do not know when an incoming call arrives because the phone does not ring. If only I had enjoyed a phone

like this in the days when I had two telephones on my
office desk!

Should you have a UK fax there is no problem in using it
so long as you have the correct plug adapter since a fax
machine does not ring.

INSURANCE

House insurance is not difficult to organise and there are
many English-speaking brokers who advertise in the
English language newspapers which are available
throughout the coastal area. Alternatively your
Spanish-speaking friend will be able to organise insurance
through a Spanish company. The good news is that if you
have relocated from a metropolitan part of northern
Europe you will be pleasantly surprised at the low cost of
insurance in southern Spain.

LOCAL AUTHORITY TAXES

Local taxes can be a bit more of a problem since the local
town hall may not be on the coast and when you go along
to sign a standing order to pay the Spanish equivalent of
council tax, you might find that communication can be a
problem. This is where your local Spanish-speaking friend
can once more be a great help. There is also the crazy
system in Spain that cheques are not routinely accepted –
the Spanish do not trust cheques!

When we first had to pay our community charges we had the invoice. We knew how much we had to pay and we knew which banks had been nominated by the local council, the *junta*, to accept these taxes. As a good, law-abiding citizen who wanted to pay the tax, I went to one of these banks armed with my cheque book from another bank only to find out after a half-hour queuing that I could not pay by cheque. The wait was half an hour because it was the day after a public holiday and the taxes had to be paid within the next two days. I was told that I could go to the nearest branch of my bank and cash a cheque and return to the first bank with cash. When I went to my bank there was a line of about 20 people. No way was I going to wait there so I decided to go to the town hall and pay there. That was not possible. You must pay at the bank. By this time the country was heading towards siesta so I had to do the whole thing over again the next day. It was frustrating but at least I had learned a lesson for the future. Have your local taxes paid by direct debit and you will save yourself this hassle.

The other reason for wishing to pay the tax by the appropriate date is the fact that in Spain, if you do not pay your tax by the due date, you are fined and interest is added for every day that the bill is not paid.

COMMUNITY CHARGES

If your property is on an urbanisation you will also have to pay community charges for the maintenance of the buildings, the communal gardens and any swimming pools. This is generally much easier to organise by standing order since the managing offices for urbanisations usually have multilingual staff to deal with the large number of non-Spanish residents who buy here. It is important that urbanisation charges are paid since a change in the law a few years ago has resulted in the possibility that if you do not pay, your property can be auctioned in your absence in order to pay the community what you owe.

We know of many people who have been very surprised that they have to pay such a charge, but what did they expect? If you have wonderful communal areas, a nice swimming pool and good maintenance of the buildings, someone has to pay. In Spain, it is certainly not the local authority.

PRACTICAL POINT
Estate agents do not always tell potential purchasers the costs involved in living in their dream property. You must ask every agent for every property you view, 'What is the community charge?' There will be a charge and you need to know how much. If you do not pay the community charge you could, under Spanish law lose your apartment.

OPENING A SPANISH BANK ACCOUNT

The first step which must be taken if you have financial affairs in Spain is to obtain a fiscal number. Non-resident foreigners should go to the nearest police station with a foreigner's department to apply for their *Numero de Identificacion de Extranjero*, NIE number. This number will be asked for in many of the financial dealings which you will need to carry out. It is needed when you pay your property taxes, when you arrange health insurance, when you buy a car and arrange car insurance and when you arrange household insurance. Bank transactions will also require your NIE number to be quoted – it is an offence for any bank to carry out transactions without reporting the NIE number of the client.

Apparently, Spanish banks have improved out of all recognition in the last few years. True, they can be frustratingly slow when you actually call into the branch, often with long slow-moving queues. They also tend to close for the day at 2 pm, particularly in small communities. As far as electronic banking is concerned, however, they are very advanced indeed. We were amazed the first time we put our cash cards into the ATM and the instructions appeared in English. Opening an account is very easy and certainly on the Costa del Sol there are always staff who speak English. That is fine but it is a bit frustrating to receive your statement in Spanish and to have to use a dictionary to translate what has been happening with your money.

It is possible to open a bank account in Spain while you are still resident in another country but it is much easier to apply in person at the bank and branch of your choice. You will need to produce proof of identity, your passport and your NIE number. If you open an account by correspondence you may be asked for a reference from your current bank.

When it comes to ensuring that you have enough money in your Spanish bank account, it is better, if possible, to transfer relatively large sums of money from the UK less frequently. If you are transferring several thousand pounds into euros you will get closer to the commercial exchange rate rather than the tourist rate.

CREDIT CARDS

Credit and debit cards are widely used in Spain although not as much as in some European countries. Spain remains a country where many transactions continue to be in cash and my comments earlier about trying to pay local rates by cheque apply also to paying for other services by cheque. Cheques are not trusted in Spain. Also your bank card is a debit card not a cheque guarantee card as it is in the UK.

The widely used UK credit cards can also be used in Spain but you will be asked for photographic proof of identity when you present the card. This can be your passport, but it is inconvenient to carry your passport with you everywhere, so a better solution is the new style UK photocard driving license. As a result of the requirement to produce photo-identity, credit card fraud is almost non-existent in Spain.

TAXES

The tax situation in Spain is quite complex and I do not propose, nor am I qualified, to go into it in detail here. Should you buy more than one property in Spain you must, by law, appoint a fiscal representative who will provide you with tax and financial services. If you so wish, your fiscal representative will take care of the organisation of payment of all your taxes in Spain. If you do not have *residencia* in Spain the tax authorities assume that you are letting your property to holidaymakers and a notional tax is therefore levied on the official value *Valor Catastral* of your property. You will also be liable for wealth tax on your Spanish assets but your fiscal representative can take care of all these taxes.

You should discuss with your financial advisors whether it would be better to be taxed in Spain or in the UK since all EU states have dual taxation agreements. As a result you only need to pay tax in one state, although this only really applies to income tax. The other tax you must pay attention to in Spain is inheritance tax, which can be very high and is not the subject of a dual taxation agreement between the UK and Spain. If you are not careful and the unforeseen happens you could end up paying inheritance tax in both countries.

> **PRACTICAL POINT**
> Do take professional advice on taxes such as wealth tax and inheritance tax at an early stage in your Spanish adventure. If you do not, you might regret it in the future.

THE POSTAL SERVICE

The final community service which I will mention here is the postal service. We all need it but in Spain it is very slow. Post offices in small towns and villages generally only open between 9 am and 2 pm (some even close at midday). There are nearly always long queues, particularly during the lead up to Christmas, and going to the post office to post or collect something can be a very frustrating experience. Luckily most tobacconists sell stamps so you can avoid the trip to the post office so long as you know which stamps to buy.

Mail deliveries can also be very haphazard. In our urbanisation all mail is delivered to one point at the entrance where someone, we do not know who, sorts it out into alphabetical pigeon holes. We have to trust that it has been correctly distributed or else we have to sift through every single pigeon hole.

The other frustration can be the time it takes for a letter to be delivered. Even letters to addresses in the same town can take a week to arrive. It is better to use the telephone or, if you have it, email.

TELEVISION

The wonders of modern technology mean that there are several satellites positioned above Europe which are capable of transmitting television in your language to your new home. To enjoy the marvels of this new technology you will need to have a set top box installed together with the appropriate satellite receiving dish. If you have retained an address back in England you can then request the coded smart card which will activate the decoding box. You will then have access to hundreds of channels of television and radio with more being added all the time. Many of the television companies who supply the smart cards such as Sky and BBC Digital cannot legally send the cards direct to an address abroad since they have copyright only for a UK audience. However, there are a number of satellite dish installation companies in Spain who can supply the cards and they advertise in the expatriate press. If you retain a UK address you can ask for the card to be sent to that address and bring it with you to Spain.

Should you buy in an urbanisation you should check what arrangements for television reception are in place. Some have a communal satellite dish which may not provide you with all the channels you would like to view and there may be a ban on private dishes being installed. You might find yourself with a surfeit of foreign language channels and very few English channels.

It is worth pointing out that a UK specification TV or video will not work properly in Spain and needs modification, except if you are going to watch British digital television. Very often it can be cheaper to buy a new set in Spain rather than have the modifications carried out since televisions are relatively cheap in Spain. Surprisingly, a Spanish purchased set will accept a UK digital signal with no problems. The only time it could be worthwhile modifying your set is if you have a very expensive TV you do not want to part with.

COMPUTERS

If you cannot live without your computer my advice to you would be to take your UK computer with you when you move. Of course it is possible to buy a new computer in Spain, although there is not the same number of large computer superstores that are found in Britain. The problem is that a computer bought in Spain will probably come loaded with Spanish software and unless you speak Spanish this might prove a problem. There are also slight changes on the Spanish keyboard as the keys have to deal with a language which has accents over some of the letters. If you use the Internet or email you will be faced with browsers in Spanish.

Having said this, I have to admit that new hardware in Spain is much cheaper than in the UK, particularly when it comes to items such as printers or scanners.

The best solution is probably to take your existing computer and have an Internet service provider installed locally by an expatriate computer specialist. When you have Internet service installed do make sure that the interface is in English and not Spanish. An example of such a programme is FastnetSpain, which I have now been using for more than a year with no problems whatsoever. Spantel is an alternative.

One accessory worth installing in Spain for your computer and television equipment is a surge protector plug. Spain does experience occasional surges in the electricity power supply and this could seriously damage sensitive equipment.

DAY-TO-DAY LIVING

Having settled into our new home the most rewarding but also at times the most frustrating experience was day-to-day living and adjusting to our new environment.

We were new to the area and we had to find out where all the necessary shops and supermarkets were located and when they were open. In fairness this was not difficult. You only need to ask the local expatriates who will be only too happy to provide the information you need.

To begin with we did find ourselves going to the supermarket armed with a Spanish dictionary. We recognised most of the food we wanted to buy – in fact many of the names were the same as in the UK – but we realised that we did not know the word for bleach, fabric softener, toilet cleaner and many of the other basics of everyday life. We had inherited a number of bottles of cleaning materials in the kitchen cupboards but even here we made mistakes. The first time we used the dishwasher we only realised after the event that we had used a cleaner which was intended to clean the dishwasher itself, not the dishes. We were also amused by the names of some proprietary products such as a brand of ground coffee called Bonka.

We needed various jobs done in the apartment and this often involved using local tradesmen who spoke little or no English. Finding suitable tradesmen was also a task which we had to do through local friends who spoke Spanish. Most of the time we got by in any dealings with tradesmen with our limited command of Spanish. There was, however, one hilarious occasion. We wanted guttering fitted to the edge of the terrace roof and we wanted to have a wood-burning stove installed in the fireplace. We mixed up the tradesmen and using sign language and a few Spanish words we tried to explain where and how the guttering should be fitted, only to have a reply in perfect English: 'We have come to fit the fireplace'. This was a Scandinavian fireplace company.

We bought a new telephone only to discover that it had been manufactured in Spain and all the instructions for use were in Spanish. Just imagine our confusion as we tried to figure out how to store numbers and all the other things a modern telephone can do while having to look up every second word in the dictionary. Unfortunately, although we live in a multinational society nowadays, not every instruction book is printed in all the European languages. We had similar problems with a toaster and an electric kettle but at least with them all you really have to do is to plug in and switch on. We also bought a new microwave and we still do not know how to use all its features. We will in time!

The other very basic thing we had to learn was the Spanish for the various programmes on the washing machine and the dishwasher since they were Spanish models.

DRIVING IN SPAIN

Once you are accustomed to driving on the 'wrong' side of the road, getting around by car is not difficult. The Spanish have a reputation for driving in the Latin way but I have not really found this to be a problem. They do drive fast on occasions and they can get a bit impatient, but I would say they are better than drivers in some other European countries and they are certainly no more aggressive than drivers in the south-east of England.

Should you take a car from the UK, it is possible to insure it on a permanent 'Green Card'. This will only allow you to take your car back to the UK for a limited number of days per year. Such insurance companies will recognise the Spanish equivalent of an MOT, the *ITV*, as evidence of the vehicle's roadworthiness in order to validate the insurance. If you intend to keep the vehicle indefinitely in Spain it would be advisable to officially export it and have it re-registered in Spain on Spanish plates. In fact by law you are supposed to register the car in Spain and officially export the car from the UK, but there are many expatriates who have driven UK-registered cars in Spain for years before they switch to a Spanish registration. The advantage of switching is that you would then have to insure it with a Spanish company and this will save you considerable expense.

We bought a car locally and have been amazed by the low cost of the insurance premium, particularly since it included roadside assistance as a normal part of the insurance cover. This is part of all Spanish car insurance. We were also amazed by the service we had from a mainstream, high volume car dealer. It far surpassed any dealer we had ever purchased from in the UK. They provided us with a detailed breakdown of service costs (much cheaper than in Britain) and fantastic after-sales service.

It is also a very pleasant experience to fill up the fuel tank in Spain since petrol is about half the cost of what we had been accustomed to – although prices are rising.

It would be my recommendation to either export a left-hand-drive car from the UK or buy a car in Spain as soon as possible, since it is much easier and safer to drive a car that has the controls on the correct side.

Car parking is also very well catered for. In most big cities and resort areas there are huge, modern car parks which are very cheap. In smaller towns parking remains free for the moment. There are occasions when cars are double parked or just abandoned, but so long as your attitude to life remains as laid back as the Spanish, this is not really a problem. One pleasant experience we had was when we discovered that in some of the smaller towns the parking meters, when they exist, also have a siesta. Between 2 and 4 in the afternoon parking is free.

KEEPING UP TO DATE WITH THE NEWS IN PRINT

You might be surprised to learn that all the English newspapers are now printed daily in Spain, so if you must read your *Times* or your *Sun* every day you can. The only difference is that the weather forecast is for Spain and not for the UK. During our first year we found that we were buying our normal newspaper virtually every day but as time passes one finds less interest in what is happening back in the old country. If anything, reading about the problems of the NHS, public transport and immigration only reinforces the fact that your decision to move to Spain was the right one. You can also buy the British Sunday papers.

In addition, there are large numbers of locally produced and printed English language newspapers and magazines, most of which are available free. These are the publications which are most useful to build up your local knowledge and to read about local news.

If you are an avid reader there are English bookshops in many of the towns, and the large department store *El Corte Ingles* has an English language section in its bookshop where you can usually buy the latest books published in the UK. We have also found Internet bookstores a very valuable resource for recently published UK books.

HOUSEHOLD MAINTENANCE

No matter where you live you will at some time need to have repairs or redecoration done to your house. This is not a problem at all on the Costa del Sol since there are many expat British who are making a living by doing household work for their fellow expats. This is good in some respects and it is certainly easier to deal with tradesmen who speak your language (if you do not speak Spanish), but should you use the services of such tradesmen you should ensure that you get a VAT receipt for any renovation work you have carried out on your home. Capital gains tax will be charged on your property should you decide to sell and move elsewhere but if you can demonstrate that certain work was necessary to modernise or renovate your home this can be offset against the CGT liability.

PRACTICAL POINT

It is worth pointing out that it can be cheaper to use the services of local tradesmen, who will charge the Spanish rate for the work, whereas some expats charge the UK rate and get away with it since the client is not aware of the fact that local rates for the job would be much cheaper. There can also be other potential benefits of using local tradesmen since they are more familiar with Spanish construction methods.

LIVING LEGALLY IN SPAIN

There is no bar to foreigners buying property in Spain but under the laws which existed until 2003, anyone, including EU nationals, needed a residence permit, *Residencia*, if they intended to live in Spain for longer than six months in succession. This residence permit was not difficult to obtain so long as you could prove that your income was above the minimum Spanish wage, you owned property in Spain or you were legally employed in Spain.

Officially anyone who lived in Spain for more than six months in any calendar year without taking out residency was liable to a fine and exclusion from Spain for up to three years, although such an event was unlikely to happen to a EU national since one of the cornerstones of EU policy is the free movement of people and goods throughout the Union. This law has not been strictly enforced and there are thousands of EU nationals who have lived illegally in Spain, more or less permanently.

It is for this reason that early in 2003 the law changed so that there is no longer a need for EU citizens to register for *Residencia*. Identification documents from the country of origin are sufficient and also allow the EU resident in Spain to vote in municipal elections. This could be interesting in the longer term since local politicians will have to start taking account of the expatriate vote. This will, of course, only happen if all expats register to vote – if they all did there would be some areas in the Costa del Sol where the expat vote would be larger than the local Spanish vote. This could make for very interesting changes in local politics in the future.

8

The Lifestyle

There are many features of everyday life in Spain to which you will have to adjust. Some are easy – some difficult.

Mañana

Mañana – tomorrow – is a fact of life in Spain. The slower pace of life leads to the situation where it is not a disaster if something is not achieved today. There is always tomorrow. When you arrange to have something done on Wednesday it might end up that it is not done on

Wednesday of this week but you need not worry it will be done next week – on Wednesday. When you first arrive it can be extremely frustrating but you soon learn to live with it and, horror of horrors, you actually find yourself beginning to fall into the same trap and you start delaying things until tomorrow. Unless a job is vitally important, does it really matter if there is a bit of a delay in completing it? In actual fact *mañana* becomes a bit of a joke.

Manaña does not just apply to delays of a few days. When you make appointments in Spain it is common for the person you have arranged to meet to turn up late. This can be annoying when you're not used to it, but before long you too will develop a more relaxed attitude to time and start turning up late for meetings. It is all part of the much more laid back Spanish attitude to life generally and when you have accepted it as part of life it certainly reduces stress. Reducing stress probably also means that you will live longer!

Siesta

Siesta is a wonderful Spanish institution. The tradition of siesta was, of course, intended to protect the population from the heat of the sun in the middle of the day but it has been carried forward to modern times. There is something wonderful, particularly in the summer months, about drawing the curtains and lying down for a couple of hours in the afternoon and many expatriates very quickly learn to appreciate siesta. It is also important to note that you can cause great irritation if you disturb people during this time.

Of course in the big cities the tradition has all but disappeared in modern times. Spain would not be able to exist in a multinational business environment if all offices, banks and shops closed between 2 and 5 in the afternoon, but siesta is still a strong tradition in smaller communities. If you go five miles inland from the Costa del Sol there is just nobody on the street between these hours. The curtains are drawn and all you see is sleepy dogs or cats lying in the doorways. Small communities become almost like ghost towns.

Siesta can have its irritations. Since the shops usually close in the afternoon even in the coastal resorts it can be annoying if you have forgotten to buy something important and there is no way you can obtain it until 5 pm. I am afraid if this is the case there is nothing you can do about it. Businesses then re-open and stay open until late in the evening.

In traditional Spain siesta has really shaped the Spanish way of life. In practice the Spanish have a 14-day week. They get up quite early and work until lunch-time. They then have a light lunch and go back to sleep for a few hours, waking up refreshed for the second part of the day, when they go back to work or re-open the shop. A quick visit to the tapas bar on the way home to stave off the pangs of hunger and then dinner very late – sometimes even as late as 11 pm. After dinner entertainment and talking can go on until the early hours of the morning before another short period of sleep to refresh the body before the next working day.

So this means that the average traditional Spaniard has two periods of sleep in every day and two periods of work or socialising – the 14-day week. It is for this reason that foreigners are warned that the Spanish can be guilty of being noisy until very late at night.

RELAXED PACE OF LIFE

Having now settled in to our new life in Spain we have had the opportunity to re-evaluate just what it is that we feel makes the lifestyle here better than it was in London or indeed in the UK generally. Having made this re-evaluation there is now no way that we would ever consider going back permanently to the UK. The way we feel at the moment we do not even wish to go back for a holiday – in some respects this is a very sad state of affairs but it is the truth. We would rather that our friends in the UK came to stay with us. So what is it that makes our new lifestyle superior?

Freedom from the stress of big city living has to be a major benefit of life on the Costa del Sol. There are fewer people around and those who are around have the time to enjoy life even if they are working. When you walk through a Spanish town people will actually say '*Hola*'

(Hello) to complete strangers. When you enter a shop or reach the check-out in the supermarket you are greeted with a smile and an '*Hola*' or '*Buenos dias*'. I have to say that this rarely happened to us in the south-east of England. The other wonderful thing is that you are greeted with a smile. Living in London I began to think that the British had lost the ability to smile.

The *mañana* attitude helps you to relax and become more philosophical. Does it really matter if there is a delay? So long as real emergencies are dealt with as they happen that is all that really matters. I have to say that real emergencies, domestic or medical, are dealt with on a much more rapid time scale than we were used to in London and at lower cost. When the main fuse blew in an apartment belonging to one of our neighbours on a Sunday evening an emergency electrician was there within 30 minutes and his charge for the call-out and the repair was only 60 euros (£40). This is probably less than the call-out charge alone in the UK.

When you first arrive in Spain the queues in the bank or the post office or other public services can be an irritation. I would be dishonest if I said that it did not bother me to begin with, but way back then I was probably still in London mode. After I adapted and started to look around only to see that delays did not seem to bother the locals, I too adapted to the fact that really there is no rush. What is the point of getting upset?

Life here is very laid back and ultimately this will probably add years to one's life. In fact we have been told that a move to the Costa del Sol could add five years to your life expectancy. I do not think that this has yet been the subject of a clinical trial but it would be interesting to find out.

THE WEATHER

The weather, the 'blue drizzle', of southern Spain definitely improves your lifestyle. Unless you actually experience it long term you cannot really appreciate how wonderful it is to wake up on more than 300 days of each year to clear blue skies and sunshine. As a self-employed consultant in the UK my office was on the second floor of the house in which we lived and was south facing. I was amazed that for most days of the year I needed to have a light switched on. This is not the case on the Costa del Sol. Apart from the fact that the sun shines most of the year it is also the quality of the light which improves life. The light of the Mediterranean gives such a luminous touch to the colours of your surroundings, a real picture postcard effect which you appreciate throughout the year.

I was worried that perhaps it might be too hot in the height of the summer but experience has shown that so long as the orientation of your property is correct the summer heat should not be a problem. There are times when it can be better to get out of the sun in the middle of the day, which you will learn to do if you live in Spain.

Remember why siesta developed! Later in the afternoon you can happily return to the sun and enjoy it. Summer evenings are wonderful. Very rarely does it feel too hot in the evening but you can still live outside comfortably – the terrace or the garden really does become an outdoor room.

An important factor in keeping the climate in southern Spain very pleasant is the relatively low humidity. I have visited countries where not only was the temperature high but the humidity was also above 90 per cent. It is only then that heat becomes unbearable. The only time that the weather can be a bit of a problem is when the hot winds blow from the Sahara. When this happens the Spanish advise you to stay indoors and close all doors and windows to keep the heat out until the wind drops.

Winter is absolutely delightful, with mostly blue skies and daytime temperatures in the 60s Fahrenheit or between 15 and 20° Celsius. At night temperatures do drop but rarely below 50° Fahrenheit (10° Celsius).

It would, however, be totally wrong to paint a picture of year-round idyllic weather. There are days when the sky is overcast but somehow the grey does not appear to be so dark. There are also days when it rains and when it rains in southern Spain it is tropical style rain. Two minutes outside and you are absolutely soaked to the skin. The roads turn into rivers and really the only thing to do is to stay indoors. The consolation is that the rain will not last and tomorrow or the day after the sun will probably be shining again. It would be almost unheard of here to experience several days or weeks of continual rain and grey skies. Without this rain the coast would not remain so green for most of the year. It is only in the height of the summer that the landscape does become a bit barren. Every living plant tends to go into a dormant phase and dries up until the autumn rain arrives. I have to say also that there are times when you almost wish for a day without sun (believe it or not!).

Suffice it to say that when northern Europe is experiencing heavy rainfall, snow or freezing conditions the Costa del Sol is probably basking in sunshine. Spain is probably Europe's sunniest country and the Costa del Sol is truly the sunniest region.

The weather alone could provide a very good reason to live here but there are still more positives which I would like you to consider.

SHOPPING

No matter where you live in the world, shopping falls into two categories: essential shopping and leisure shopping. Both are well catered for in Spain.

Turning first to essential shopping for the everyday things of life, the choice in Spain is almost bewildering. In the smaller towns you will find small supermarkets which are fine for everyday shopping and even there you will find an amazing array of fresh produce, but to really experience choice you have to visit one of the hypermarkets which are to be found usually on the immediate outskirts of larger towns. The first thing you notice in these shops is that the counters selling fresh food are far bigger than the counters displaying frozen food. Frozen and convenience food is only really there for the non-Spanish clients – *los turistas*. The Spanish themselves still tend to buy fresh food, which is one of the reasons that eating in Spain remains a healthy pursuit, at least for the locals.

Fruit and vegetables

The displays of fruit and vegetables are amazing. Virtually all of the items on display are loose, allowing you to personally select what you want and then have it weighed and priced. Spanish hypermarkets do not insist on regulation size and shape apples, pears or tomatoes. What you buy here has probably been grown in the farms behind the coast. It is fresh. It is almost certainly organically produced and it is so cheap.

If you really want to, it is possible to buy fruit and vegetables which have been imported but the real bargains are to be found by buying what grows in this region when it is in season. In season fresh asparagus is so cheap that you would not consider it to be a luxury vegetable as it is in the UK. Tomatoes are in season throughout the year as are all the other salad vegetables.

There are root vegetables in profusion (these tend to keep better in Spain if they are refrigerated otherwise they go soft very quickly). You buy garlic by the bag not by the individual bulb and onions are almost giveaway in price.

Fruit is amazingly good. In season (November to early summer) oranges are so cheap it would be sacrilege not to buy them and invest in a juicer so that you have a constant supply of fresh orange juice. (I still find it amazing to see holidaymakers buying processed orange juice for their children while on holiday – do today's children only know how to enjoy synthetic products?) Lemons are around 1 euro for a kilo and the local mandarins and grapefruit are also delicious, for this region is one of the major producers of citrus fruit in the world. The strawberry season is from mid February until the end of April and in season one tends to buy strawberries by the box, two or three kilos at a time. They are delicious because they have been picked when they have ripened on the plant not picked while unripe and transported to the UK to ripen off the plant in cold storage. Following the strawberry season cherries come into their own in the late spring or early summer. This part of Spain is not a good region for growing apples or pears so you have to be a little bit more careful when selecting these fruits, but nectarines and peaches grow very happily.

There is also a very good selection of more exotic fruit such as pineapples, kumquats, kiwi fruit, pomegranates and custard apples, all of which are grown locally. The best time to buy bananas is when the crop from the Canaries is in season. Bananas imported into Spain from further afield often have very little flavour.

Fish and shellfish

Never in my life have I seen such a selection of fish and shellfish on the fish counter even in a specialist fishmonger in the UK. This should not be a surprise since Spain consumes more fish and shellfish than any other country in Europe. Fish in Spain comes either from the Atlantic or from the huge reserves of fish in the Mediterranean.

When you first visit the wet fish counter in the hypermarket it would probably be advisable to take with you a dictionary or a Spanish food shopping guide to help you with the display of fish of all shapes and sizes. Space does not permit me to list all the various fishes which you might see on display but among the best buys here are tuna which is caught off Cadiz in the Atlantic waters, *cazon* (often called rock salmon in the UK) which is related to the shark family, *boquerones* (anchovies), *dorada* (gilt headed bream) which is a delicious fish, *lenguado* (Dover sole but also found in Spanish waters), *robalo* (sea bass), *merluza* (hake), *rape* (monkfish – delicious but not one of the world's prettiest fish), *salmonete* (red mullet) and *sardinas* (sardines – fresh sardines bear no relationship to the tinned variety and are excellent barbecued). The traditional dish of sardines in Malaga is *sardinas al espeto* – sardines barbecued on skewers over hot coals, often on the beach.

Turning our attention to shellfish, on the wet fish counter there is an equally large selection which ranges from clams, crab claws (*boca de la Isla*, the single claw of the fiddler crab), calamares, octopus, scallops and lobster and prawns of all shapes and sizes. These are only the shellfish you will recognise. In addition you will find sea anemones, cuttlefish, spider crabs, sea urchins and sea snails. You may be tempted to try some of these more exotic shellfish.

Meat and poultry

The selection of meat and poultry in the hypermarket is not so bewildering to the new arrival and all you really need to know is the name of your chosen meat in Spanish. *Ternera* is generally young beef – *buey* signifies that the beef has come from an ox (male). *Cordero* is lamb while *carnero* is mutton and *cerdo* is pork. *Pollo* is chicken and *pavo* is turkey. Generally you will recognise the various cuts of beef and other meats but I should point out that the designation *filete* is not a fillet steak but a name given to any slice of meat which is off the bone.

In the butcher's section of your chosen hypermarket you will also find a good selection of game in season, a huge selection of cured meats and hams and many different varieties of Spanish sausages. Spain is particularly famous for its mountain produced cured hams which are often purchased whole. They are absolutely delicious.

Should you prefer to buy your meat in the British way you will find that in the coastal areas there are many enterprising British butchers who have opened shops where the cuts are the UK variety. Many of these butchers also make their own British style sausages and import back bacon should your tastes run to a typical English breakfast on occasions.

Olive oil

Spain is the world's leading producer of olive oil and some of the best flavoured olive oils in the world come from this country. As a result the hypermarket shelves are filled with a huge array of different oils and it is therefore necessary for you to know which ones to buy and how to use them. That is if you decide to buy your oil in a commercial store. If you so choose you can make a visit direct to the mill – the *almazara* – taking along with you a 5, 10 or 20 litre bottle to be filled or you can buy it from an olive oil depot.

Olive oil has been called the world's healthiest cooking oil and is often credited with contributing to the good health which the inhabitants of the Mediterranean region often enjoy. Which type of olive oil should you choose?

Extra virgin olive oil is produced from the first cold pressing of the olives. It is the most expensive but it can also have the most characteristic flavour so it tends not to be used as a cooking oil. It is perfect for salads or spooned over potatoes, cooked fish, vegetables or pasta or even bread, the classic *aceite en pan*.

Virgin olive oil is also unrefined but heat is allowed in the extraction process. It is fine for fried foods such as fish, chips or fritters. It is also very useful for sautéing.

Olive oil (*aceite de oliva*) has been refined and is the blandest in flavour but it is perfect for everyday cooking and is fairly inexpensive. Since we moved here it has become our staple cooking oil.

I have to say that since moving to Spain I have used no other oil other than olive oil. We have also adjusted to the Spanish tradition of sprinkling olive oil onto bread as an alternative to butter and it is a delicious alternative.

Wines and the harder stuff

For wine lovers Spain is paradise. Throughout the country wine is produced ranging from the full blooded reds of Rioja through to the sweet whites produced in some parts of Andalucia. The first real surprise is how inexpensive wine can be when it is not subject to the swingeing taxes imposed on wine in the UK. The price can range from less than £1 per bottle for basic everyday 'plonk' up to many euros per bottle, but even 'expensive' wines can be a lot less than the equivalent of £10 per bottle, and that will buy you exquisite examples of the winemaker's art.

The other real surprise which awaited us was Cava, the well-known Spanish sparkling wine made by the champagne method. Purists might disagree but the taste of a good Cava is almost indistinguishable from the taste of Champagne and many ordinary individuals would be hard pressed to tell the difference. The real surprise was the discovery that perfectly drinkable, everyday Cava can be bought for less than two euros a bottle in some of the hypermarkets. Cava comes in two varieties, brut and dulce. The former is the one which tastes most like champagne.

If you like a tipple of the harder stuff, spirits are also surprisingly cheap compared to British prices, with litre bottles of gin, whisky, vodka and brandy at around five or six Euros. Sherry, which is of course produced in Jerez de la Frontera in Andalucia, is also very reasonably priced. One surprise is that, unlike the UK tradition, sherry in Spain is drunk chilled.

Street markets

Shopping for food can also be done at the street markets which exist in many of the towns in the region. The larger towns have markets which are open every day for food. Prices in the markets are likely to be cheaper than those in the hypermarket. The street market will often be host to local small producers of fruit and vegetables and if you buy from them you are cutting out any middle man in the retail chain. The same applies to buying from the many fruit and vegetable stalls which can be found at the roadside in country areas. We use these and at one of them we also buy our eggs while the chickens which laid them are walking around, free range, at our feet.

The markets are also very good for essential leisure shopping. The various street markets are a good source of resort wear, beach towels, domestic towels, sheets and pillowcases, shoes and many other everyday articles. The quality is generally very good and the prices are very reasonable indeed. A pointer to value probably comes from the fact that many local people use the market for their shopping.

Some markets are also a good source of Moroccan artefacts such as earthenware, outdoor light fittings and articles made of brass or other metals. There are stalls to be found which sell rustic style furniture which is perfect for older style properties and second hand furniture – all at very good prices but be prepared to barter. The market may also be the source of original paintings and other types of art. Many of the markets are very good places in which to buy rugs and mats. Most of those sold in the market are of north African origin but today they are often made of synthetic fibre so they tend to be very inexpensive and you can barter. They are relatively hard wearing and are perfect to warm up the marble or tiled floors of your home during the winter months. When they need cleaning they are cheap enough to throw away and be replaced with new. (Should you want to buy very good quality Berber rugs you can always go on a day trip to Morocco and visit the souks.)

Consumer durables

Should you need to shop for electrical goods for the kitchen you will be pleasantly surprised by the low prices compared to the same brands in the UK. Televisions, video recorders, audio and DVD players are considerably cheaper than the equivalent in the country you have just left.

Spain is also well served by DIY warehouses which have a very wide stock of all the things you need to improve your home at very reasonable prices. Many of the items you will find in outlets such as Leroy Merlin have great style at an affordable cost and you really can do all your DIY shopping under one roof.

For me it is the style of many of the items you find in specialist shops in Spain which I find amazing. There are shops selling absolutely beautiful, stylish furniture which were it to be on sale in London would cost considerably more.

What you do not tend to find in the south of Spain are the large out-of-town furniture superstores which have sprung up in the UK. Furniture is still a reasonably specialist commodity. Having said that, around the expensive areas of the coast there are some very good shops which sell second hand furniture, and some items are very good indeed. To people with a lot of money in places such as Marbella or Puerto Banus, redecoration does not just mean painting the walls and changing the curtains, it means that everything is changed. Some of this very expensive furniture therefore finds its way onto the second hand market.

In the bigger towns you will find department stores such as El Corte Ingles which offer high fashion, high style and I regret also quite high prices compared to the other places where you might choose to shop. Nevertheless you can spend a few pleasant hours just browsing in these stores. One positive thing about such stores, at least in the areas where there is a large expatriate community, is the fact that they import the best selling books from the UK. I cannot recall any of the large stores in London having a Spanish section in their book departments.

The only real problem with respect to leisure shopping is dealt with in more detail later, which is that the resort areas can be limited in the number of shops they offer.

EATING OUT

This is one of the real delights of Spain. Forget about the English restaurants where you will find typically British food. They exist but only in the major tourist areas and frankly you would need to be fairly unadventurous to choose to eat in such establishments. Having chosen to live in Spain you really should try Spanish restaurants and start to eat in the Spanish way.

The first absolutely typical Spanish food outlet must be the tapas bar. Tapas are delicious bite-sized appetisers which can either be hot or cold. They are very typical of Andalucia. Since the Andalucians tend to eat dinner very late the tapas bar is a pleasant place to snack before the main meal of the evening.

Tapas can be as simple as plump, well spiced olives, toasted almonds, wafer thin slices of serrano ham, chorizo, mature cheese or prawns in their shells. *Tapas de cocina* (cooked tapas) include croquettes of cheese and ham, battered prawns, goujons of crisply fried fish, roasted peppers and various salads from the simple to the exotic. Other cooked tapas are meatballs in tomato sauce, tiny pork cutlets, prawns sizzled with garlic and chili – the famous prawns *pil-pil* – clams or mussels a la marinière, anchovies with garlic, Moroccan style kebabs and of course Spanish omelette (*tortilla*) to list but a few.

Should the individual tapas be too small for your appetite you can ask for larger portions called *raciones*, but I should warn you that several *raciones*, particularly if they are fish or shellfish based, can prove quite expensive as a light meal.

The ideal choice of restaurant for a delicious and leisurely lunch is the *chiringuito*. These are the very simple and inexpensive beach restaurants where the specialty is often seafood in its many guises. The restaurants themselves are very unassuming but the quality of food is usually very high. The best value is often a plate of mixed fried fish or wonderful fresh sardines cooked simply on a hot plate (*sardinas a la plancha*). There is nothing more pleasant than sitting under the canopies of a *chiringuito* close to the sea. This is especially true in the winter months when you remember that the population of northern Europe has to remain indoors to escape the winter cold.

Another option for lunch is to try out some of the other typical Spanish restaurants. By law restaurants have to offer a set lunch shown on the menu at a fixed price. You will be amazed to be offered a simple three-course meal with bread and a glass of local wine for not much more than the cost of a meal in a fast food restaurant in the UK.

Other restaurants worth sampling are *ventas*. These are typical local Spanish restaurants, usually family run, found at the roadside and very common in the country areas. They are very Spanish and a working knowledge of the language can be a help particularly the further you travel from the coast. What many of these *ventas* offer are simple meals prepared in the traditional method and they too can be incredible value for money. Just ask around wherever you choose to live and you will soon be recommended the best *chiringuitos* and *ventas* in the area.

Of course there are also some very upmarket restaurants, particularly in the coastal resorts, where a meal can cost a lot of money. Many of these restaurants will have Spanish dishes on the menu but the cuisine is likely to be reasonably international in its overall choice of dishes. In my opinion such restaurants are best kept for the odd special occasion unless you have a lot of disposable income to spend on eating out.

With the increasingly large expatriate and tourist community you will find Chinese, Indian, Thai, French and Italian restaurants in profusion and of course American style burger and pizza establishments, including the ubiquitous McDonalds. If you really must eat in the English way, particularly for Sunday lunch, many of the big hotels and some UK oriented restaurants offer a Sunday brunch which includes a carvery. Here you will find a very large selection of starters of all types and for the main course there will always be roast beef, turkey, pork and lamb cooked in the traditional English style. Such places are absolutely ideal for those with a huge appetite since you can return to the serving counter as many times as you care to. We do know people here for whom Sunday is not Sunday unless they have their English roast lunch. However, we tend to eat in Spanish style restaurants often and really value the exceptional value for money which they offer.

HOME COMFORTS

Wherever you buy your home in the south of Spain it is likely to be ideally designed for the climate here. Should you buy in a typical Spanish town the streets will be narrow and the windows of your home small. The walls will be thick. All these features keep out the heat in the summer and keep the house warm in the winter.

Should you buy a modern property you will probably have wide glass patio doors opening onto a terrace designed for outdoor living in the summer months. We certainly live on our terrace in the summer. Such properties can have some problems in the summer if the terrace faces south and you may have to devise ways of keeping the sun out of your indoor living area through the use of shutters or blinds. If you face south you may even need to install air-conditioning.

Whatever type of property you end up living in the floors will almost certainly be tiled. The most common tiles are teracotta or marble, although in properties built about 20 or 30 years ago you may find tiles which are more like ceramic tiles with a marled or speckled effect. Tiles are wonderfully cool in the summer months and marble especially seems to stay cool even on the hottest days. Teracotta tiles are a bit warmer underfoot and seem warmer in the winter months, although this may be an illusion since they are darker in colour. The coolness of marble floors can be a bit of a problem in the winter period. We do need to find as many rugs as possible to cover up the marble. I suggest you bear in mind when viewing properties that if you like two properties and one has a log burning fire while the other does not, go for the one with the fireplace. You will not regret it. We find that we welcome being able to light a real fire in the evenings from mid November until early March. There is also absolutely no doubt that logs are the cheapest form of heating in Spain (and the most attractive).

Continuing the winter theme we have also found that it was a very good idea to bring duvets with us from the UK. They are definitely necessary from November until March. In the spring and autumn you will probably get away with a sheet and an American style comforter while during the summer months a single sheet will probably suffice.

GETTING AROUND

Traveling around in Spain is basically a delight. Of course the traffic is heavier in the cities and in the larger towns and the locals complain bitterly about the traffic jams. Their comparison is, of course, with the general levels of traffic encountered locally. Traffic jams in Spain bear no relationship to those seen on the M25 around London or the M5/M6 around Birmingham.

We had been warned about the traffic in August during the peak holiday season but I have to say that after the new dual carriageway coastal road opened there has really been no problem. Motorways generally are a dream come true, with very little traffic even at peak periods, since the only people who use them are those who want to move quickly from A to B and are prepared to pay the toll charges.

So far I have been talking about the traffic on the main roads but if you move onto the minor country roads the traffic is amazingly light, even in the height of the holiday season. Go five kilometres inland and there is virtually no traffic on the roads throughout the year at the western end of the Costa del Sol. Getting around is a pleasure and I hope it stays like that in the future. There is usually little opposition to road improvement schemes when they are needed.

Public transport, where it exists, appears to be very good. There is a regular bus service along the coast from Malaga to La Linea and while it may not be frequent, so long as you know the time the bus leaves from your nearest stop it is likely to be on time. The coaches are comfortable. The fares are low and every coach is air-conditioned.

Similarly the rail network along the coast is not extensive at the moment but apparently it is going to be extended from Fuengirola to Estepona and on to Algeciras. Trains run on time and are reasonably priced – unlike in the UK! The long-distance train services are very good indeed and soon Malaga will have a high-speed link to

Madrid. Seville already has such a link. There is even a suggestion that the high-speed link from Madrid should be extended to Estepona.

9

The Cost of Living

It is all very well talking about the wonderful lifestyle in Spain but we had to think very carefully about whether or not we could afford to live in this paradise in our new semi-retired state. We had to think not only about our level of income now but also in the future. My income is fixed and in fact might even fall if the stock markets fail to rally a bit in the future. Julian's pension is index linked but it dies with him unless the EU rules concerning transfer of pension rights between unmarried partners who are financially dependent on each other are changed.

Obviously we also built into our sums the fact that at some point we will be able to add the UK state pension to our income forecast. It is necessary to consider future potential income at the same time as thinking about the cost of living.

LIVING WELL AND CHEAPLY

Experience has now shown that the cost of living in Spain is considerably lower than in the UK, especially if you choose to live like the locals. If you own your home and have no debts it is surprising how little money you need to survive, and if your income is reasonable you will find that you can live very well in Spain.

Property is cheap compared to most parts of the UK. Even if you choose to rent rather than buy, rents are much lower. Food is definitely cheaper but we have found that if you want to buy some of the food items we were accustomed to in London, they can be very expensive since they have to be imported. Wine and other alcoholic drinks are considerably cheaper and cigarettes are half the price one has to pay in the UK. We rapidly learned that Spain is not one of the world's larger producers of beef so beef is expensive but if you enjoy pork and chicken they are much less expensive than in the UK. All types of pasta and rice are cheaper, as well as fruit and veg, which keeps down our cost of living.

Our bills here are around half the London cost for cooking and water heating. Gas is bottled and it is certainly cheaper. A gas bottle costs us around £7 and even when we were cooking and heating water using gas in our first apartment a gas bottle lasted up to six weeks.

As I explained earlier we have found the cost of eating out much lower, especially if you go to restaurants which are favoured by the local Spanish population. If you go to smart restaurants aimed at holidaymakers the bills can be almost as high as in London. The problem is that many of these restaurants are run by expats for the British and they tend to charge what they would have charged back home. The customers often do not bother to check out the Spanish restaurants to discover that they could be eating out a lot cheaper.

We have found that house insurance, car insurance and, as discussed later, health insurance are all much cheaper than in London. We also save money on car repairs and maintenance and household repairs so long as we take on the services of Spanish tradesmen. Even with a new Spanish bought car from a mainstream dealer the servicing costs are a fraction of those in the UK.

WHAT COSTS MORE?

So Spain sounds like a paradise – is anything more expensive? Quality clothing is probably more expensive than the equivalent in the UK, although if you live on the coast you tend not to wear very smart clothes. For most of the year we live in shorts and t-shirts and wear sandals bought in the market or in the hypermarket for a few euros.

Since we first moved to Spain relative prices have changed. Initially we thought that almost everything we looked at was cheaper than we were accustomed to but at that time the pound was strong and the euro was weak. That situation is changing and the euro has gained almost 12 per cent against the pound, which means that real prices are 12 per cent higher compared to sterling. Unfortunately most of our income is in sterling so we have to take this into account and it is probably the only real worry we have for the long term. A major reduction in the value of the pound could seriously affect our disposable income.

It is impossible to state that the cost of living is x times lower than in the UK since the cost of living is dependent on what each individual chooses to buy. I can, however, say that there are many expatriate pensioners who own a property in Spain and manage on the UK state pension. They may not be living in the lap of luxury but they do have a better lifestyle on a relatively low income than they would have had if they had chosen to remain in the UK.

PRACTICAL POINT

If you are reaching retirement age or planning early retirement contact the Overseas Department of the Department of Social Security and get a pension forecast. This is especially important if you have been contributing to SERPS. If you have worked constantly since leaving school you may be pleasantly surprised at the pension you will receive when you reach retirement age and it may not be necessary for you to pay another penny into the fund.

10

The Hidden Delights of Spain

Of course Spain is a popular holiday destination for the
British and other northern Europeans but it is a pity that
so many travellers come here only for sun, sea and
sangria. There is so much more to experience than just a
beach or poolside holiday with a bit of wild entertainment
in the evening. There is the wonderful history and
tradition to experience, which is of course well
documented in the various travel guides on sale. What I
will describe in this chapter is not the stuff of the travel

guides but the many wonderful everyday experiences which can only be fully appreciated when you live in Spain throughout the year.

CIVIC PRIDE

I suppose that one of the first things to strike me in Spain was the real sense of civic pride which even the smallest town seems to have. The streets are clean and free of litter. The houses when occupied are kept well painted on the outside and the owners fill their balconies, terraces and window boxes with a riot of brightly coloured flowers. Seafront promenades are being restored and even in towns which are not really significant tourist resorts there is ample and elegant streetlighting. The other thing you notice is the almost total absence of graffiti. In areas which are recognised as tourist attractions, believe it or not, the owners of properties repaint them at their own expense virtually every year.

The absence of litter was demonstrated in a practical way when we went to the 'Three Kings' procession in Estepona during the Christmas period. The procession takes place on the evening of the 5th January and really is the major festival of the Spanish Christmas period, and of course a public holiday. The procession was spectacular and took quite a long time to pass by. The celebrations were accompanied by the people on the floats throwing sweets to the assembled spectators which, of course, led to quite a lot of rubbish on the streets. Imagine our surprise to find that the procession was followed at a respectable distance by the local rubbish collection team who were clearing the streets of all evidence of the procession. I think it unlikely that their equivalent in the UK would do this on a bank holiday at 10 in the evening.

Incidentally, domestic rubbish collection is organised differently in Spain. There is no collection from individual households. The collection is from large communal refuse bins which means that we have to carry our refuse to the collection point, but in return the collection point is emptied more often – once a day in the summer months.

DAY-TO-DAY PLEASURES

Just driving around on everyday business is a real pleasure in this part of Spain. We usually drive along the coast road to the next small town to visit the local English butcher, the three garden centres which are to be found there and the log yard where we buy our firewood in the winter. Ordinary everyday chores can become a source of real pleasure and wonder. Some days the sea is so blue it looks as if someone has poured blue dye into it. There is one particular bend in the road when suddenly on a clear day almost the entire coast stretching towards Gibraltar comes into sight, and in the distance the most wonderful view of the Riff mountains in Morocco. I have to say that I never really thought that I would see Africa on an everyday visit to the butcher's shop.

Driving in the opposite direction our view is of the entire bay of Estepona right along the coast to Marbella with the surrounding mountain ranges. Such views are not what brings the tourist to Spain but they certainly brighten up everyday life and make you feel very good to be alive.

The other simple pleasure is rising every morning to blue skies and our wonderful view over the golf course towards the mountains and the sea. At the end of the day when the dogs are taken out for their last walk the skies are usually amazingly clear and you are aware of the brilliant canopy of stars which are so much a feature of Mediterranean life. Added to this is the sound of the crickets in the undergrowth.

THE WONDERS OF NATURE

The tourist who comes to the south of Spain during the height of the summer may return home thinking that the landscape is parched and dry. It is only when you live here that you experience one of the true delights of nature. At the end of the summer the first rain for several months falls. Within a few days the wild flowers are growing again and soon the countryside is a mass of colour. The seeds have remained dormant over the summer but they have always been there.

We were horrified one day in the middle of the summer when a JCB arrived and cleared land fairly close to us prior to redevelopment of the site. Clearing it in July turned it into a dustbowl. Fortunately the developers did not obtain planning permission for the intended buildings so the land was left empty. When the rain arrived the road outside our apartment became a sea of mud for a period as the soil washed off the hillside, but this lasted for only a very short period. The JCB had successfully spread all the dormant seeds in the soil and soon after the rain nature reclaimed this land. It rapidly became a sea of wildflowers. Unfortunately this land has now been built on!

Keeping to the subject of plant life, when you drive along the valley of the Guadiaro river you are immediately struck by the fact that almost as far as the eye can see there is nothing but citrus groves. In season these trees are absolutely laden with oranges and lemons. This valley has now been recognised as one of the major citrus growing regions of Andalucia and the growers are allowed to put stickers on the fruit stating its origin. The harvest is so extensive that many of the growers sell oranges by the sackload at the side of the road – at the price they charge, they are almost giving them away.

As you climb further up the valley the next sight which takes your breath away is sunflowers filling the fields. This is another local crop used for sunflower oil production. The hills on the opposite side of the valley are home to hundreds of black bulls which are still bred in Andalucia for the bullring. I appreciate that many people are against bull fighting. I suppose that I fall into that category, but as I read in one local publication here, which is more desirable? In the UK bullocks might live for two years in cramped conditions before they are sent off to the abattoir, whereas in Spain they graze the fields for five years before being taken to the bullring for their moment of glory. I realise that the fight will always end with the death of the bull but at least he has the opportunity to fight back to some extent and may in fact inflict severe injuries on the matador.

We have also been struck by the wonderful variety of birds we see all around, which attract many keen bird-watchers to the area. Although we are not ornithologists we were still so fascinated by the profusion of birdlife that we had to go out and buy a book on European birds so that we could identify as many as possible. We are only one kilometre from the coast but we have kestrels and buzzards soaring overhead. There are colonies of green parakeets who have made their home in Spain and who arrive regularly in the gardens of our urbanisation to strip the dates off the palm trees. A pheasant has taken up residence in our gardens and if you go a bit further inland into the hills and mountains, without too much difficulty you will see eagles soaring majestically overhead.

Further down the coast towards Gibraltar we were amazed to see that the local authorities had actually put platforms on the top of the telegraph poles to provide a place for storks to nest. During the breeding season it was fascinating to look out for the chicks sitting on the top of the nests waiting for mother to come back with food. There are many rare birds which only breed in this part of Spain, and we discovered that the new toll motorway actually has a tunnel to take the road away from a particular spot where some very rare birds have colonies.

FIESTAS AND *FERIAS*

The average holidaymaker may be lucky enough to experience one of the many *fiestas* or *ferias* which take place throughout the year in Andalucia. It is, however, unlikely that anyone will actually come here expressly to experience a *fiesta*, with the exception of the *Semana Santa*, (Holy Week) celebrations in Seville. It is only when you actually live in Andalucia that you really begin to appreciate *fiesta* and how important it is to the local population.

During a *fiesta* the real character of Andalucia comes to the fore, with singing and dancing, prancing horses, religious icons and food and wine in abundance. Many of the festivals can trace their roots back to pagan times – the Church took on board the old traditions and built those pagan festivals into the Christian calendar. As in Britain, Easter is associated with the arrival of Spring and is always held on the first Sunday after the full moon following the spring equinox. Christmas in turn is closely linked with the winter solstice which has been celebrated for centuries.

Christmas in Spain is a two-week celebration which begins with *Nochebuena* (the good night) on Christmas Eve. On New Year's Eve, *Nochevieja*, people meet each other in the town square and eat the 12 grapes of good luck, one for each chime of the clock. Finally on the evening of 5th January the country celebrates the Feast of the Three Kings, Epiphany. This is the occasion for major processions through the streets and is the traditional night for Spanish children to receive their presents.

This Christmas cycle of *fiestas* is followed in many towns and villages with Carnival, which is the last *fiesta* before the period of abstention, Lent, which leads up to Easter and Holy Week.

Holy Week is a major *fiesta* in many of the towns of Andalucia. The processions often start as early as Palm Sunday and continue throughout the week, building up to a major procession through the streets of many towns on the evening of Good Friday. In this procession the sacred icons from the local church are carried through the streets of the town preceded by the brotherhoods of the penitents in their characteristic hooded outfits. The icons are followed by a procession of veiled women walking barefoot through the streets.

The best known *Semana Santa feria* is that in Seville. This
has become a major tourist attraction for the city and
hotel rooms can be very difficult to obtain, such is its
popularity. The events start on Palm Sunday when the
whole of the population of Seville appears to have taken
to the streets, and the bars are open throughout the day
and night. The actual processions are organised by the lay
brotherhoods, *cofradias*, who also own the effigies which
are paraded through the streets in procession. Each day
during the week there can be up to 11 processions, all of
them beginning and ending in the church where these
effigies are kept, although all the processions pass before
the magnificent cathedral. On Wednesday the Sevillians
stop work and the next two days are public holidays. This
is a signal for the celebrations to really get into top gear
and they reach their peak on Good Friday. Saturday is
relatively quiet and on Easter Sunday, rather than more
processions, the major event of the day is the first
bullfight of the season. About two weeks after the
Semana Santa processions the Seville *feria* begins.
This is the signal for the women of Seville to dig out
their flamenco dresses and with the entire city on holiday
and in festive mood the party lasts for a week.

Christmas and Easter are, of course, the two major
Christian festivals of the year, but in Andalucia the *fiesta*
and *feria* season does not end with these festivals. Every
town and village holds an annual *feria*, usually during the
summer months. These *ferias* are held simply for the
enjoyment of the local population but there are also the

other *ferias* which are associated with certain dates or
events.

One of the most spectacular is the *Fiesta de San Juan*
which is held on Midsummer's Eve. In the coastal areas
this is spectacular. Huge tableaux are built on the beach
with imagery of family scenes, demons and devils. Along
the beaches barbecues are lit in the sand and sardines are
barbecued on long spits. On the stroke of midnight the
tableau is set on fire and as the flames die down members
of the local population run through the smouldering
embers into the sea to purify the spirit. This is usually
followed by a huge fireworks display and various bands
playing for dancing in the street for most of the night.
What really hits home at this *fiesta* is that virtually the
entire population of the town appears to turn out for the
festivities. In our nearest town, which by anyone's
standards is quite small, this *fiesta* is really spectacular.

We live in a grape growing region where there is a strong
wine producing economy and this leads to yet another
fiesta – the *Fiesta de la Vendimia* – which celebrates the
grape harvest. Not to be outdone, other communities hold
harvest festivals to celebrate whatever produce they
happen to produce locally.

Coastal areas have their annual processions to honour the
Virgen del Carmen, the patron saint of fishermen, and
these processions culminate in spectacular sea-borne
processions of the effigy of the Virgin. Increasingly,

neighbouring towns are combining their resources in order to make this *fiesta* even more spectacular. Away from the coast, many towns and villages have their own *fiestas* to honour a local saint. These are often called *romerias* after the tradition of gathering wild rosemary, *romero*, along the route of the procession. The largest of these *romerios* is held on the edge of the Coto Dõnana national park at Whitsun when around a million people gather to watch the *Romerio el Rocio*.

As a tourist you could be lucky enough to find yourself in Spain at a time when one of these events is taking place. If you live here all the time the various *fiestas* and *ferias* soon become part of your normal life and you begin to participate along with the locals.

PEACE AND QUIET

Fiesta is by no means peaceful, but the one thing which is striking in this part of Spain is the absolute peace and quiet which can be experienced. You will not find it in the large urban resorts along the coast but you only need to drive a few miles inland and the activity and buzz of the coast disappears totally. Park your car and just walk in the countryside and you are immediately struck by how calm everything is. Of course you hear the sounds of nature, the birds singing, strange rustlings in the long grass made by some unseen creatures, the noise of the breeze in the trees overhead, but at other times there is almost complete silence. Go higher into the mountains and often as you walk across what appears to be grass you will find that you are actually walking across a carpet of fresh herbs which release their delightful scents into the air. Stop for a few minutes and just listen. In the mountains you are likely to hear the distant ringing of the bells hung around the necks of the goats.

You do not even have to go very far from the coast to experience this peace. Where we live on the high ground close to the sea the quietness of the evenings and mornings is stunning. Should you wake up in the middle of the night you hear almost nothing.

This aspect of Spain is one of the most amazing of the hidden delights of this country.

11

Gardening in Spain

One of the most rewarding pastimes in Spain has to be gardening in whatever form it takes. Whether you are lucky enough to have several acres of land, a small garden or only a terrace on which you can place some colourfully planted containers, gardening is one of the real pleasures here.

Yes, there is a winter season in Spain. It does rain and when it does you may see rain of the stair rod variety but

this is what keeps the trees green and the plants alive.
The climate is subtropical and the sun really does shine
throughout the year. Even if your garden is restricted to a
terrace there are always plants which will flower 12
months of the year; as one species ends its flowering
season another species takes over. All it needs is careful
planning for constant colour.

Because of the climate, gardening in Spain is different.
Many plants which you probably grow as houseplants in
the UK will grow quite happily outdoors here and grow
to a much greater size than they ever would as a
houseplant. The best advice is to look around the
established gardens in your neighbourhood and see what
is growing happily and then check out the garden centres
in order to find these plants. The last thing you should try
to do here is to recreate an English country garden. Such
a garden survives well in England because of the UK
climate but it can be very difficult to grow some of the
plants you might have been accustomed to in the old
country in the climate of southern Spain.

Should you allow yourself to be bitten by the gardening
bug in Spain you will very rapidly realise that you are
gardening in paradise.

PLANNING

Whether you have a large garden or just a terrace,
planning is an important part of the process. Only when

you live here will you realise how much time is spent outdoors, so you need to plan for an outdoor life. This means that you will want views of your results but you will also want to create space so that you can sit among those results and enjoy them. You need to plan for year-round interest and colour and for relatively easy maintenance. After all, you probably do not want to spend all your time gardening. Should you plan to leave Spain during the height of the summer, either because you want to avoid the annual holidaymakers or because you want to escape the heat, this will also affect your choice of planting.

If you have a proper garden you should plan for a terraced area to link the house to the garden. This fulfills two purposes. The first is that a hard surface immediately next to the house protects the lower parts of the outside walls from moisture and the second point is that it will give you a living space immediately outside the door. You also need to take into account the orientation of the terrace. If it faces due south you will need to provide shade in the form of an awning or a pergola to provide shelter from the strong summer sun. Whatever the orientation of the garden, overall you should try to provide sunny and shady seating areas throughout.

Having decided on a plan or at the very least having decided on where the seating areas are and where you want to plant, the next decision you need to make is what to plant. You should aim for a planting scheme that will provide you with year-round colour and interest. This is something which the professional landscape gardener will always consider. The ordinary gardener will often be seduced into buying those plants which are in flower and look best in the garden centre the day they visit. In this way it can be very easy to end up with a garden which only flowers at a certain time of the year.

To help you plan I will describe some of the options open to you in choosing plants for your garden in Spain.

PLANTING FOR COLOUR

Spain is a country where you will find a riot of colourful flowers wherever you travel. The Spain of the guidebooks really does exist, with whitewashed houses and flowers cascading from the iron window grills, the terraces or simply clustered around virtually every front door. The most common plants used to provide this colourful display are geraniums, petunias, busy lizzies and begonias, although there are many other plants which can also be used.

Geraniums

For colour there is almost nothing to beat geraniums in the Spanish garden or on the Spanish terrace, whether they are in pots or in the soil. They come in so many colours and so many types, including the common geranium (zonal geraniums), ivy-leafed geraniums, trailing geraniums and the scented leafed varieties. The latter, although they do not flower so profusely, are wonderful for the scent they give out when you brush against them.

Spain has an almost perfect climate in which to grow geraniums and with very little effort they will flower throughout the year. They grow well in sun although they appreciate shade from the searing heat of the midday sun. They also grow in light shade. The soil should be kept on the dry side and should be well drained. To encourage flowering, dead-head on a regular basis and feed with special geranium fertiliser or with liquid fertiliser designed for tomatoes. They do grow very large and need to be pruned from time to time but if you are growing geraniums in pots on the terrace the best idea is to prune some in spring and the others in autumn. In this way you will have flowers throughout the year.

Petunias

This very colourful plant is ideal for pots, planters or hanging baskets and also has a very long flowering season. They are available in a many colours and the flowers last for a long time since they do not have the scourge of rain which so easily destroys petunias in Britain. We have also been struck by the fact that many of the varieties sold in the garden centres in Spain have a very strong scent.

Begonias

Once again a plant which is available in many different

colours and which grows very well in containers or
hanging baskets. They too benefit from the lack of rain
which can destroy the flowers but they do need to be
watered on a fairly regular basis. Looked after carefully,
they will continue to produce flowers in profusion for a
very long time. You also have the choice of the smaller
flowers of the *sempervivens* variety or the dramatic large
flowers of the tuberous varieties.

Busy lizzies

Another wonderful plant for the terrace pots. It flowers
continuously through the summer but the one thing you
do need to be a bit more careful about with this plant is
to avoid full sun if possible. Busy lizzies do need a lot of
water in the Spanish climate or they just flop over and
die, but looked after properly they will reward you with a
profusion of flowers and colour for almost 12 months of
the year.

Other plants for colour

Carnations grow very well in Spain and are almost the
national flower – the image of the flamenco dancer with
carnation held between the teeth is a very common one.

For very sunny positions in the soil or in planters,
portulaca is a wonderful plant to grow in Spain. It is a
summer flowering annual with fleshy, succulent leaves
and multi-coloured daisy-like flowers which only open in
full sun. Another daisy-like flower which is very easy to
grow in Spain is *gazania* which needs very little attention

once established but produces a profusion of flowers of many different colours. In fact nearly all daisy-like flowers grow extremely well in Spain. If you have the space you must plant sunflowers, which in the right surroundings can be very dramatic indeed.

Another popular pot plant back in the UK is the cyclamen. I have to say that we never really had great success with cyclamen in London and they never lasted for very long as a house plant. On our terrace in Spain we can grow them like weeds and they flower for months. They are available in the garden centres here in a multitude of colours with plain or variegated leaves and definitely should not be ignored. They do need shade.

Many other familiar flowering plants from your UK gardening experiences include antirrhinums, marigolds, lobelia and stocks, which all grow here. A visit to your local garden centre will introduce you to many other flowering plants to ensure that your Spanish garden or terrace is never without flowers.

ROSES

Roses are the archetypal flower of the English country garden but I have to say that they really come into their own in the climate of Spain. The rose is not new to Spain. There is evidence from Arab manuscripts that roses have been grown here for 800 years. With the right attention roses flower from March until Christmas with no interruption at all. The flowers last for longer since they are not subject to the sudden downpours which can destroy the flowers in an English garden.

Your Spanish roses can be planted in the garden in rose beds or among mixed planting. Some varieties will grow well in pots on the terrace. The walls of your house can be covered in climbing or rambling roses. Choose the varieties with a strong scent and you will be amazed how the scent lingers in the air during the warm, still, summer evenings.

The only attention roses need once they are established is dead-heading on a regular basis to encourage new blooms to open, regular feeding to support strong growth and vigourous pruning in January to encourage strong new growth for the next season. Do not be afraid to prune very hard almost down to ground level, ensuring that the bud immediately below the cut is pointing outwards. Hard pruning is necessary since your plants will have a very long growing season and they will soon reach a good height again.

PLANTS FOR SCENT

The long, warm summer evenings in Andalucia absolutely call out for fragrant flowers to fill the night air with their perfume. As well as jasmine and roses which are described elsewhere in this chapter there are many other plants which fit this category.

One plant which cannot be ignored is the *Dama de Noche*, *cestrum nocturnum*, which must find a place in every garden or be grown in a container on your terrace. It is deciduous and in terms of its foliage it is not really very interesting to look at but in summer and autumn it produces clusters of relatively inconspicuous yellow-green flowers which produce the most incredible perfume after dark. Grown on a terrace they will fill the terrace and possibly even your living room with their perfume. This wonderful perfume has an added advantage in that it deters mosquitoes. This plant should not be ignored.

A very easy but beautiful plant which grows well here is the gardenia. The common gardenia, sometimes called cape jasmine, is an evergreen plant which can grow into a bush or even a small tree. It is an attractive plant even when just in leaf but when the white to cream double flowers appear the perfume is exquisite. The flowers are also very long lasting on the plant and our gardenias often flower twice in the year. The only problem with growing gardenias here is that the tap water is rich in lime and gardenias do not like lime so you need to use bottled water for irrigation.

If you have a warm sunny terrace you could try growing *stephanotis*, whose white, waxy, scented flowers are often included in bridal bouquets in the UK. It is a climber and can be trained around a cane structure set into the pot. Unless the terrace is very sheltered *stephanotis* may not overwinter even in Andalucia since the recommendation in the gardening books is not to let the temperature drop below 59° Fahrenheit. But here the beauty of terrace gardening comes into its own: bring the plant indoors in the winter months.

Freesias are another heavily scented plant which you can grow very easily in Spain. The corms can be planted in the autumn for spring flowering or in the spring for autumn flowering. They grow so easily and so profusely that it is difficult to believe that a tiny little spray of freesia in England can cost so much. Once established they will flower year after year.

Above I have described some of the scented plants which you would probably not have been able to grow outside in your home country, but there are others with which you may already be familiar, which will also grow in Spain. Among these are wallflowers, honeysuckle, hyacinths and various species of lily.

CLIMBING PLANTS

Bougainvillea

Everyone who has visited the Mediterranean coast or indeed any other region of the world which is hot or subtropical will remember the dramatic sight of a wall or a pergola covered in bougainvillea. We tried to grow it in our south-facing garden in London on several occasions but every time we tried it died in the winter.

Basically it cannot take temperatures lower than 50° in the winter.

Whatever your gardening aspirations are, in Spain you must grow bougainvillea, either against a warm, sunny wall or in a large container on the terrace. The most common variety is the deep purple colour but there are other varieties with colors ranging from white through to orange and salmon.

This wonderful climber grows rapidly and needs to be well tethered to its support. It flowers for a very long period but it does respond well to serious pruning. Most importantly it should not be overfed or over-watered. Follow these simple rules and you will be rewarded with a riot of color in true Mediterranean style.

Clematis

Clematis grows well in Spain but it does need a bit more care since the roots need to be in the shade and the flowering branches prefer the sun. As a result it is not so well suited to planters or pots in Spain, since they can get quite warm in the summer, but it will grow well against a sunny wall if the roots are well protected by thick planting around the base. I should point out that your chosen sunny wall should not be subject to midday sun.

Grape vine

The grape vine is obviously one of the main commercial plants in Spain both for fruit and for wine production but it is also a wonderful climber to grow over a pergola so that it provides you with shade in the summer. You need to make sure that you look for a climbing vine in the garden centre since the vines intended purely for fruit production are kept low to the ground and pruned hard every year. Vines need to be watered well in the spring and summer but need very little water at other times of the year.

If your vine is intended mainly for shade you only need to prune lightly in the autumn, cutting off the shoots which are hanging downwards from your pergola or arbor.

Jasmine
Space permitting this is one climber which you cannot ignore in your Spanish garden. The common jasmine bears a huge number of highly scented flowers and is indispensable for scent in the garden during the warm summer evenings.

Passion flower
This is a very vigourous climber which grows extremely well in the Spanish climate. It has the advantage of being self-clinging by means of tendrils so you should provide it with the necessary framework to cling to as it grows. The well-known purple flowers are produced constantly from the new growth throughout a very long period. There are also white and red varieties.

So far I have been talking about all these plants as climbers but there are some which can also be regarded as trailing plants. We grew a passion flower very successfully in full sun from a raised planter at the edge of the staircase to our first apartment in Spain and I have to say that it looked wonderful spilling down the white walls of the staircase.

Wisteria

This is yet another climbing plant which would seem to be inextricably linked with an English country garden. The sight of a wisteria-clad cottage is quintessentially English and yet it is also a climber which grows remarkably well in southern Spain. In fact it grows so well here that it can flower twice in the season, in spring and then again in late summer.

Wisteria does need a good strong support since a fully grown plant can be very heavy, such is the profusion of leaves and flowers. It is ideal for pergolas but an established wisteria will also twine its way up the trunk of an old tree to dramatic effect. The plant will grow in fairly ordinary soil but it does welcome a fair amount of watering.

BUSHES

There is such a large choice of bushes and shrubs that grow well in Spain it is almost impossible to make a limited choice to describe here. If bushes are what really interest you it would be worthwhile buying a specialist book on Spanish gardening. I propose to list only the most common or those which are very easy to grow.

Oleander

The oleander is one of the wild bushes of Spain. As you drive along the roads there are often huge clumps of oleander at the roadside and this immediately tells you something about the plant. It needs very little maintenance once established. Oleander has waxy leaves which are very drought resistant so it needs very little watering. The only thing you need to be careful about with this plant is the fact that it can grow very large if it is not pruned on a regular basis. Six metres high and four metres wide is not uncommon for one plant. The most common colour is pink but there are also white, coral, blood red, salmon and yellow varieties and a mixed colour planting of oleander can look very dramatic if you have the space. It is extremely hardy and very easy to grow. In our communal gardens we have several very large oleander bushes which were offered to the community by a former resident who moved to a new property where he inherited several well-established large bushes. Our gardeners went along and dug them up (not easy to do!), brought them back and replanted them. For the first season they looked a little bit sad but by the second season they had taken off and they are now growing very well indeed.

Hibiscus

This is not a native plant in Spain and in fact originates from eastern Asia and China, the south east of the USA and Hawaii, but it has acclimatised to the sub-tropical areas of Spain like a native. Hibiscus grows quickly and can grow to a very large size indeed but if it gets too big just cut it back to the size you want and it will take off again. No Spanish garden should be without this spectacular bush, grown for its dramatic flowers which are either single or double and can be up to five inches across. It almost seems a waste that each flower only lasts for a day either on the plant or when cut, but the flowers are so profuse that every day the bush is covered in blooms. In the right environment it flowers all year round.

Hibiscus does need to be pruned to keep it flowering properly and long stems should be cut back early in the year so that you avoid having fewer flowers just at the end of these long stems.

Angel's trumpet (datura)

This is a really spectacular bush which produces long, hanging, tubular flowers which are fragrant in some varieties. Datura will grow well in a sunny, sheltered position out of direct, strong winds. It should be pruned once a year and it does need a fair amount of water. It will grow in a container but you do need to remember that it is potentially quite a large bush so even when container grown it needs space.

Lantana

Lantana is another common bush in this part of Spain. It is often referred to as *la bandera* since the colours of the flowers of the most common variety are the same as the colours of the Spanish flag. In the UK lantana is often grown as a bedding plant and as soon as the winter arrives it dies. In Spain it can grow to great heights as a hedge or as a bush and is virtually indestructible. It is possible to cut it almost down to ground level and up it grows again to reach the same height as before. It seems to grow with very little help from the gardener; in fact if it is given too much fertiliser it will actually stop flowering. It is also very undemanding with respect to watering.

Apart from the common variety with its orange, yellow and red flowers there are also other hybrids of different colours, blue, purple and yellow being the next most common. It needs to be pruned occasionally to remove dead wood but given a reasonable amount of care, lantana is another of the Spanish bushes which will offer you a very long flowering season.

Cistus or rock-rose

Cistus is yet another of the wild bushes of Spain which can be seen at the roadside or in the countryside. Cistus grows very well in hot, dry areas and once established it survives with very little attention. It is invaluable for stabilising dry banks since the roots will bind the soil together and help prevent soil erosion during periods of heavy rain.

Broom

Spanish broom is often grown in British gardens but in Spain it tends to grow much better. Spain is its natural habitat in fact. In the spring the mass of yellow flowers which appear on this plant is truly amazing.

Fuchsia

In your Spanish garden or terrace you will be able to grow fuchsias very well and here they are really a shrub rather than just a pot plant or terrace plant. Once established in a spot which has some protection from the midday sun you will find that the flowering season can be very long and it is not unusual to see fuchsias flowering in Spain in January.

Fuchsias flower on young wood so if you want to have the maximum number of flowers it is necessary to pluck out the growing tip of the plant on a regular basis to encourage new growth at a lower level. Plants can be grown very easily from cuttings. Since the fuchsia in Spain flowers almost constantly, to keep your fuchsias growing you need to take cuttings on a regular basis because the parent plant will ultimately exhaust itself and stop flowering, then your cuttings can take over.

Other bushes

There are many other bushes and shrubs which will grow well in Spain in containers or in the garden. Among these are hydrangeas, tamarisk, spiraea, the bottle brush plant, philadelphus and ceanothus.

SCULPTURAL PLANTS

One of the true delights about gardening in Spain, even if you are restricted to container gardening on the terrace, is the large number of dramatic foliage plants, often familiar as pot plants in Britain, which will grow quite happily outside. Some of these plants do have flowers but they are usually grown for the dramatic effect of their foliage which will remain the same throughout the year. Many of the following plants have been included in this section as plants but in reality some could also be classed as trees.

Ficus

Back in the sixties no British household was complete without a rubber plant. For those whose fingers were not particularly green this plant often ended up as a stalk with a couple of glossy green leaves at the top. You will not have this problem in Spain. The rubber plant, *ficus elasticus*, grows vigourously in the open air and in fact it will branch readily and ultimately could end up as a very large tree. All varieties including the variegated types grow equally well.

We never had any success in London when we tried to grow the weeping fig, *ficus pendulus*, which always ended up losing all its leaves and looking very sorry for itself. Basically it had to be grown as a house plant and it does not like central heating. On our terrace in Spain we have container grown weeping figs which are flourishing and have not lost any leaves at all. Given time and the right conditions the weeping fig will grow into a sizeable tree, but if you want to keep it in trim it can be pruned quite radically to keep the height down.

The other members of the *ficus* family such as the creeping fig, *ficus pumilis*, also thrive in this climate. It can actually be very effective to plant a weeping fig in a large container and surround it with creeping figs which will trail down the side of the container.

Philodendron

There are many plants that, although listed as house plants in Spanish gardening guides, we have found will grow happily on a terrace in containers. A terrace, especially a covered terrace, could be thought of as half-way between outside and inside. One such plant is *philodendron*. The dramatic large leaves are particularly effective in the corner of a terrace and if the terrace is sheltered you could try growing *philodendron* alongside *monstera deliciosa*, the cheese plant for a particularly dramatic effect.

Sanseveria

Mother-in-laws tongue, that well-known house plant in more northern regions, will grow very happily on a sheltered terrace in Spain. It is especially effective as part of a group of containers with its striking variegated, striped leaves.

Clorophytum

The spider plant is another common indoor plant in
northern Europe but once more it can be grown on a
sheltered terrace in the south of Spain. It is particularly
effective in a hanging basket or supported by a wrought
iron plant stand so that the cascade of new plants which
are formed on long arching stems can be seen to full
effect.

Poinsettia

I have included this well-known plant in this section
rather than in the flowering section since the familiar red
'flowers' are in fact bracts, a type of leaf, so strictly
speaking the poinsettia is a foliage plant. It grows very
happily outside in Spain and in many towns the local
authorities fill their public flower beds with them at
Christmas. Spain is the only place where we have been
successful in keeping poinsettias alive so that they flower
the following year. All that is necessary is to take the
potted plants and plant them in a flower bed or a planter.
When the last bracts have dropped off, cut the plant
down to almost ground level. You can surround the cut
back plants with other plants to provide summer interest
so long as the surrounding plants do not need too much
water: geraniums are ideal. When new growth starts to
appear, water more frequently and you will be rewarded
with possibly even better poinsettias than you had the
first time round. The bracts will not be so large because
they have not been forced for the Christmas season but
the colour will be richer and the plants stronger.

In Spain the poinsettia has the ideal conditions to produce its coloured bracts since their successful production requires a period when there is almost an equal period of dark and light during the course of a day and this is exactly what we have in Spain during the winter months.

Schefflera

This very well-known foliage house plant for colder climates will grow very happily on the terrace or in the garden in Spain. In the garden it will ultimately grow into a tree and can grow up to 40 feet high. However, if it is kept in a container the growth will be restricted. It is absolutely ideal for an area of dappled sunlight and will also grow in shade. The one thing it does not like is full sunlight in the height of the summer.

This is one of the benefits of container gardening. In summer you can move the shade loving plants out of direct sunlight to somewhere more sheltered and bring the sun lovers to the forefront.

Strelitzia

I have included this dramatic plant in the sculptural section although it would be equally at home in the flower section. Its common name is the bird of paradise flower. The very dramatic flowers, which really do look as if an exotic bird has landed on the plant, are very sculptural indeed and it makes a wonderful specimen plant in the middle of a mixed border or in a container.

The long leaves are also very attractive even when there are no flowers.

There is also a giant form of *strelitzia* which has black and grey flowers. Although the flowers are less striking the plants themselves grow to 15 or 20 feet high with long cut leaves. This species really gives a tropical feel to the garden if you have the space to accommodate it.

Anthurium

This beautiful plant is usually referred to as the flamingo flower in the UK, where it is sold extensively as a house plant. It is very beautiful in leaf but when it flowers and throws up bright red 'flowers' which are actually spathes with a central flower element, it is a truly dramatic plant. Even in Spain it may be categorised as a house plant but we have successfully grown it for a long time on the terrace even during the winter months, when it continues to flower almost constantly. It is worth trying as a terrace plant but not as a garden plant where it might be too exposed in the winter.

Aloes and agaves

These beautiful, sculptural plants will grow very happily in the strong sun of Andalucia and produce a really tropical effect, whether in the garden or container-grown on the terrace. Since they are succulents they need very little water but they will reward you with spectacular spikes of flowers at various times during the year. Some throw up striking red spikes in December and January while others have yellow inflorescences in the spring or summer. The Spanish often grow an aloe vera close to the kitchen door so that in the event of a cut or a burn they can rapidly cut off a slice of the leaves to treat the wound with aloe vera juice.

Agaves are very similar in appearance to aloes but many species are considerably larger. There are agaves with leaves up to six feet long and these are truly spectacular plants. The one major difference between the aloe and the agave is that agaves do not flower every year and when they do flower the rosette of leaves of most species dies soon after leaving the plant to propagate by means of the offshoots which have already formed around the base of the parent plant. To propagate the plant it is very easy to pull out these offshoots and plant them in another part of your garden.

Kentia and other species of palm suitable for terraces

The Kentia palm, which is used so much by interior designers as a strong focal point in a room, will actually grow very happily on a terrace in Spain so long as it is sheltered from direct sunlight. This plant can really make a bold statement on your terrace or in your courtyard and help to create a truly sub-tropical atmosphere. It is long lived and can grow to great height. It is also helped by the fact that it does not grow too quickly.

When we were having our London garden landscaped we did try to include hardy palms into the terrace planting and we also had palms in the living room (the Kentia was one of them). Our outdoor palms survived the winter but they did not grow terribly quickly in the British climate. We had them transported to Spain and they are now on our terrace, where they have really taken off in terms of growth. In fact during the growing season you can almost measure the growth of new leaves on a daily basis. The following palms can be recommended strongly should you be able to find them in a Spanish garden centre.

They include the lady palm, *rhapis sp.*, which we grew as a houseplant in England but which is thriving in a shady corner of the terrace. This palm does not like sun since it came originally from the shady forests of China, but if you have the right location it is a very dramatic plant with its long stems and flat tufts of shiny leaves at the top of each stem. In a container it does not grow too quickly but it can potentially reach a height of 5–15 feet.

We have also had great success with the jelly palm, *butia capitata*, a slow growing palm from the cool areas of South America. It is slow growing in terms of height but it does produce new leaves very readily and these are wonderfully long and arched. Altogether a very elegant plant.

The final palm which is thriving on our terrace is *chamaedorea microspadix*, a very attractive palm related to the well-known parlour palm and which originated in the Mexican rain forest. It has long bamboo-like stems with large arching leaves and will grow very well in a sheltered courtyard or on a terrace if protected from strong sunlight. Once again you have to remember that ultimately this plant could reach a height of 10 feet.

One more plant which many would consider to be a palm but is actually a totally different species is *cycas*, the sago palm. It is actually one of the most primitive plants still to be found in the garden. It dates back to the age of the dinosaurs and later evolved into the conifer family. The sago palm is a very dramatic plant with its thick stem and crown of leathery, palm-like leaves. It will grow quite happily in full sun and needs average watering. If you have the space you should certainly consider buying one of these spectacular plants but I should warn you that they are among the most expensive plants you will buy in Spain.

Space only permits me to mention a few of the palms which we have found to grow successfully on our terrace but there are many more, and since most palms originated in sub tropical or tropical areas of the world it is worth trying out any palms which you find attractive when you visit the garden centre. I will deal with the tree sized palms in the next section.

TREES

The landscape of southern Spain is very different from the British landscape when it comes to trees. This is not a country of deciduous forests with dramatic autumn landscapes as the leaves change colour. In fact many of the trees with which you may be familiar will just not grow successfully in the heat of Spain. They need a cold weather period to flourish. Nevertheless there are many beautiful and interesting trees which do grow well in Spain, so if you have a garden there is a wonderful choice. What is wonderful is that many trees are really grown for their flowers as much as for their foliage. If your garden is small you need to choose very carefully from the large number of possibilities and do remember that unless the shade from the tree is important you should not plant too close to the house. Tree roots can cause a huge amount of damage to house foundations and also to swimming pools as they search out water.

Mimosa

Even in the smallest garden you need to find space for one or two mimosa trees. There are varieties which flower in the winter and if one of these is planted alongside the common variety which produces masses of yellow, fluffy, fragrant flowers often several times a year, you will have a regular display of blossom from this beautiful tree.

Conifers

The tree which has developed such a bad reputation in England, the *leylandii*, grows extremely well here, but it is better grown as a specimen tree rather than as a hedge which will obscure your view totally after a few years.

Should you want to plant a tree which will become a landmark in a few years' time, the Norfolk Island pine with its distinctive upswept branches will fit the bill. Should you have high ground in your garden crowned with a ridge, a line of narrow Italian cypresses can be most effective. They are easy to grow and once established they will last a lifetime.

The rubber tree and the weeping fig (described earlier) will also grow into trees in this climate. Another example of the difference between a house plant in Britain and a tree in Spain.

Flowering trees

One of the most spectacular flowering trees in the south of Spain is the jacaranda. This beautiful tree has wonderful feathery foliage but the main reason for growing it is the display of blue, pea-like flowers in the middle of summer which last for weeks and attract the bees.

One tree which is not grown as widely as it should be on the Costa del Sol is the frangipani or *plumeria*. The common frangipani, *Plumeria rubra*, has beautiful rose-pink to deep red or copper clusters of flowers from summer to autumn and really is a most dramatic sight. It is deciduous and is a native of Mexico. It will grow in Spain in a sheltered position since it does not like temperatures to drop much below 50°F. It is worth trying if you can find it in a garden centre locally.

The bottle brush tree, *callistemon*, is another dramatic flowering tree which should be considered. This tree, a native of Australia, produces masses of brush-like flowers in the summer and the common red variety is a real eye-catcher as a specimen tree.

Magnolia is another very good tree for your Spanish garden but the first thing which strikes the former inhabitant of northern Europe is that magnolias in Spain are a bit different from those in the north. In the UK, magnolias flower on bare wood in the spring before the leaves appear. This is because they originated in the colder climate of China, whereas the magnolias which grow in Spain originated in Florida. The *magnolia grandiflora* is evergreen and can reach great heights – up to 75 feet in the right position – and it produces the most wonderful large white flowers which can be almost 10 inches across from late summer to autumn. This magnolia can also be trained against a wall and almost treated as a semi-climber. If you have the space, do plant one.

Fruit trees

Fruit trees are wonderful in the Spanish garden since not only do many produce a wonderful display of blossom but the blossom is then followed by wonderful edible fruit which you can use in the house.

The almond tree is wonderful for a small garden. It will provide you with a fantastic display of flowers in late January or early February but if you plant the right variety it will also provide you with a good crop of almonds later in the year. In order to produce almonds it is usually necessary to plant two trees so that they cross-pollinate but if space is at a premium you can plant both trees in the same hole. Almonds have an advantage over many other fruiting trees in that they do not require a huge amount of water.

All the citrus fruit trees grow happily in Spain. They all need very well-drained soil to succeed, but if your garden cannot support this you can grow them in raised beds or even in containers. In fact a very good talking point can be the need to go out to the terrace to pick a lemon to complete your gin and tonic.

All types of citrus fruit trees share the same requirements with respect to soil and also to the fact that they do not need too much water, so do not plant them close to your sprinkler system. They all produce wonderful blossom in the spring which is followed by the fruit. When carrying fruit they are equally showy. The native orange to this part of Spain is the Seville orange, which grows very easily. Unfortunately the fruit is on the bitter side and is really only suitable for making marmalade, but other sweet oranges, mandarins and clementines will also grow very well and if you have enough space it is possible to plant several different varieties which produce fruit at different times so that you prolong the fruiting season.

Alternative fruit trees

In your Spanish garden it should also be possible for you to grow peaches and nectarines, which are members of the cherry family. You can also grow cherries and plums. The real wonder of growing fruit here is that you can leave it on the tree until it is ready to eat. You do not need to cut the fruit before it is ripe and allow it to ripen off the tree.

If they appeal to your taste, figs, pomegranates and pears are also possibilities in your fruit garden.

Olives

The tree of the Mediterranean! Since before Roman times the olive has been native to this region. There is only one species and it grows in sharp, well-drained soil in full sun. The olive is very slow growing but should you be lucky enough to inherit one in your Spanish garden it is a wonderful specimen tree. Should you happen to buy a country property with an established ancient olive grove you are very lucky indeed. For me the olive typifies this part of the Spanish countryside. Flowers are produced in the spring and are followed by the production of the fruit. The olives are green at first but when fully ripened the fruit turns black and can be shaken from the tree and collected. For centuries the olive has played a major part in the economy of this part of Spain, whether for the fruit or for the wonderful oil produced from it. In fact Andalucia is one of the major regions of the world for the production of olive oil.

Should you be fortunate enough to buy an olive grove along with your country property you can invite the locals who collect olives to come to your property and collect yours. These will then be taken to the local press and you will receive in return one third of the oil produced from them, while the other two thirds will be sold by the locals who collected the fruit. An old tradition which continues in the way it has done for centuries.

Palm trees

No Mediterranean garden (or even terrace) should be without a few palm trees. There is not the space here to describe the various palms which could be grown in your own sub tropical paradise – that is better left to the specialist gardening books – but a visit to your local garden centre will demonstrate just how many different species are available. I should point out that established large palms can cost quite a lot of money but the effects can be worth it. Alternatively you can start out with younger versions of the same plant and wait for them to grow. Some species do grow quite quickly and after a few years you will have the palms you want but your initial investment will have been much lower.

It should be pointed out that once a palm has become fully established and has grown to a respectable height it is not a low maintenance plant. In order to keep them looking their best they need to have the old dead growth cut off and this is a job for a specialist. He will come along and cut off the dead fronds leaving a well sculptured, pineapple-shaped base to the green fronds above. In order to do this he needs to shin up the long trunk armed with a suitable cutting tool. This is definitely not a job for the amateur and palms will cost you money in the future. Not only do the dead fronds need to be cut off but sometimes it is necessary to trim off the fruit as well. This applies particularly to the date palm which can be seen everywhere on the Costa del Sol. If your date palms are close to a swimming pool the fruit definitely needs to be removed otherwise you can cause real damage to the pool filters.

Another plant which, although it is not a palm, is often associated with palms and is also very strongly linked with the Mediterranean region is the yucca. As a pot plant in the UK, yuccas rarely reach large proportions. In the south of England they will grow in the garden but if they reach more than 10 feet in height this is unusual. In Andalucia they grow quite easily and quickly to 20 to 30 feet in height and they branch much more often. They throw up their spectacular spikes of white flowers on a regular annual basis and do look wonderful. One word of warning, however: the yucca has a very invasive root system and the roots can damage neighbouring property so great care is needed in choosing a suitable site. In our urbanisation we had to cut down a yucca because its roots were threatening to destroy the retaining wall of a raised bed and another had to be removed and the roots destroyed as it was threatening to break through the concrete wall of the swimming pool.

Yuccas and aloes are often planted together in a typical Andalucian rock garden.

Cacti and other succulents

The hot sun of Andalucia provides an ideal environment to grow cacti and many other succulents which you could not even have considered growing outside in northern Europe. If you have a dry arid part of your garden you can turn it into a desert garden with cacti large and small. Some will grow almost as big as trees and the really wonderful thing about cacti here is that grown outside in natural surroundings they flower and produce seed. Some of the tree-like cacti in our communal gardens have just appeared from seed produced by some of the original plants which were planted. The other benefit of growing cacti is that they need little maintenance and very little watering so a cactus garden is ideal for the gardener who is absent for part of the year.

The absentee gardener can also choose from a great number of succulent plants, all of which thrive even without regular watering.

THE SPANISH PATIO

A patio or a terrace is an ideal way in which to indulge your interest in gardening while at the same time creating a pleasant and relaxing environment for outdoor living.

The true patio is a legacy of the Roman occupation of Spain which was subsequently developed during the Moorish occupation. Traditional houses were built around a central patio or courtyard – in fact they are often referred to as patio houses – and this courtyard was open to the sky. Many old village houses still enjoy this feature. It provides an open air but cool environment in the height of the summer and ideal conditions to grow many plants.

A similar effect can be created even in a modern apartment in Spain, where the terrace will often be open to the world on one or two sides with a roof to protect it from the elements. This is very different from apartment construction in many other countries where apartments have balconies rather than terraces.

Patios or terraces give a wonderful feeling of being both indoors and outdoors at the same time and with careful planning you can create something magical. The choice of containers in which to grow your plants is limitless and a visit to the garden centre or the local *ceramica* will provide you with a bewildering choice at prices which will surprise you. You can choose anything from plain terracotta, carved terracotta, glazed pots either in a single colour or painted, cast iron containers and many others. The price range can be anything from the surprisingly inexpensive to the ridiculously expensive. You will find statuary which you can mix in with your pots and cast iron stands to lift them off the ground or iron wall brackets to enable you to create your own hanging gardens.

There are many benefits to be obtained from container gardening. Plants which might not otherwise grow in your garden because the soil is wrong can be grown in pots since you can give them the right conditions. As plants pass their best period in terms of interest they can be moved to the back of the group of containers and those coming into their interesting period can be moved forward. Plants which might not survive the mild Andalucian winter can be taken inside for a couple of months when the temperatures, particularly overnight, are at their lowest. The walls of the terrace can be trellised to allow you to grow climbing plants which will provide colour and interest without necessarily taking up too much of the valuable living space.

On a really small terrace you can still use the walls for plants and add special brackets to the edge of the terrace to hold window boxes. Even window boxes planted with geraniums create a more pleasant environment and you will also be doing something very Spanish.

One feature you really should try to include in the planning of your outdoor room is running water. If you look around there is a good choice of water features ranging from tiled, Moroccan wall fountains right through to large free standing fountains which could be incorporated into a larger patio or terrace scheme. Since you are creating an outdoor room even the smallest space can include a table-top fountain which is often designed for use in a conservatory. In the heat of the summer the sound of running water is very soothing.

FINALLY . . .

In this chapter I have only touched on some of the basics of a Spanish garden, patio or terrace. There is almost no limit to what can be achieved in the wonderful Andalucian climate, whether you have a small terrace or acres of land. All it needs is imagination, the right plants and the climate of Andalucia.

12

Healthcare in Spain

In the run-up to our removal to our new life in Spain there were many friends in the UK who asked whether we were worried about healthcare in Spain. In the UK you always have the NHS to look after health needs and the British have always been told that the NHS is the envy of the world. If you can afford the high prices of health insurance in the UK you can always opt for private care. At the time of moving we were both basically fit and apart from the fact that Julian suffers from asthma we had no immediate problems to worry about. But we had to accept the fact that we are getting older and we might need to call on Spanish healthcare in the future.

STATE PROVISION

When you reach retirement age in Spain, as an EU pensioner you will qualify for the same heathcare provisions which exist for the local population without charge for GP consultations, hospital care or the necessary drugs. Until that time it is advisable to cover yourself with private health insurance.

Many UK expatriates have depended in the past on the E111 form which was available on demand from Post Offices. This form was intended to provide emergency care for EU citizens in another member state when on holiday. It was not intended to provide healthcare for an individual who lived in another member state all the time and in fact using it as such was illegal. However the E111 was replaced in January 2006 with the European Health Insurance Card – the EHIC – which will still be available by application through the Post Office. This new card is only intended for UK residents who spend six months of the year in the UK and six months in another member state – if you spend more than six months of the year outside the UK the EHIC is technically illegal and you should make other provisions for healthcare. Note that E111s which were issued in the past may no longer be valid after January 2006.

If you are leaving the UK to live permanently in Spain you can apply to the NHS for an E106 form which will allow your healthcare costs in Spain to be charged back to the NHS for an agreed period – usually 18 to 24 months – giving you time to shop around and make the appropriate (and legal) provisions for your healthcare needs.

PRIVATE HEALTH INSURANCE

We wanted to be totally honest, legal and above board when it came to healthcare provision so we decided that we would pay for private health insurance in Spain. We received very good advice from our many friends who already lived here, which helped us narrow down our choice of insurance provider, and we arranged to see the local representative. A few days later he came to see us and explained the services on offer and the costs. He took us through the application form and we signed on the dotted line. Our private health insurance costs a fraction of what it would have cost in the UK from one of the big name companies and it offers far more. Since I am under 60 my premium is about one fifth of the UK cost and due to the loading for someone over 60, Julian has to pay just over a third of the equivalent UK insurance. Having said that there really is no equivalent UK insurance since the cover here provides for GP and hospital care, ambulance service and one visit to a dental hygienist each year. The policy covers care anywhere in Spain and also provides for emergency healthcare while traveling outside Spain.

This insurance service provides the insured with complete freedom of choice with respect to the doctor you choose to see so long as the chosen doctor is linked to that insurance company, and most are. The system works on the basis of a book of vouchers which you take to the doctor when you visit. You sign to verify you have had a consultation and the doctor signs and returns the voucher to the insurance company, which then pays him direct. It works very well and it is a wonderful thing to have private GP care. When you ring for an appointment it may be possible to see the doctor the same day and if not then the next day is almost certainly possible. When you do reach the surgery your consultation will be as long as it needs to be – indeed it can last for up to an hour – and there are no queues in the waiting room. We have been very fortunate to find a GP who trained in Spain and then moved to England where he trained further and worked. Needless to say his English is perfect and we feel very confident with our choice of GP.

A potential downside of the Spanish system is the fact that private GP care means that you have to pay for prescriptions, but this is not as frightening as it might seem. As I mentioned earlier, Julian has asthma but his basic medication is available here without prescription from the pharmacy and costs only the equivalent of £3, which is considerably less than the cost of a UK prescription. Basic antibiotics are also available without prescription and often the pharmacist can be a very useful first port of call when you do not feel well. His advice can often save the need for a visit to the doctor. Even when it comes to more expensive drugs the cost need not be prohibitive. Julian's asthma had become a bit unstable and he needed something a bit stronger to prevent symptoms. Our Spanish GP recommended a drug which has completely transformed his asthma and taken away all symptoms. He was apologetic that the drug was expensive but in real terms one month's treatment costs the equivalent of a meal for two in Spain in a reasonable restaurant. Our doctor said that it would be difficult to prescribe this drug in the UK since the NHS was not really in favour of its widespread use due to cost.

HOSPITALS

Hospital care in Spain is infinitely better than it is in England. In the larger towns and cities the hospitals are modern, well equipped and spotlessly clean. Waiting lists for most hospital procedures are much shorter and follow-up care is better. The negative in Spain is that generally speaking preventative medicine is not as well developed as it is in some other countries in the EU. It is often the hospital doctor who will advise on how to prevent a condition happening again but this is after the event. This branch of medicine is, however, developing and the Spanish authorities are beginning to realise that it can be more cost effective to prevent the need for hospitalisation in the first place.

AMBULANCE AND PARAMEDIC SERVICES

Although we are covered very well by our private health insurance we also decided to subscribe to what can only be described as another insurance policy but one which does provide immense peace of mind. All along the Costa del Sol there is an emergency ambulance service called *Helicopteros Sanitarios*. It operates on the coast and to a distance of about 15 kilometres inland. In an emergency you can call for an ambulance which will arrive very quickly and bring an English speaking doctor and nurse to your home where they will treat you on the spot. Not only will they come to your home but they offer the same service wherever you are – at the roadside, on the beach, in a restaurant or on the golf course. The ambulance has a separate driver and if the call-out is potentially a life-threatening emergency the driver will call for the helicopter ambulance service which will transport you to hospital together with the same doctor and nurse who will provide emergency treatment on the way. The following case histories show just how effective this service is in an emergency.

One would expect a service such as this to be expensive but in actual fact it costs just over £1 per week per insured person. This small sum brings immense peace of mind and as a result many EU pensioners who qualify for free healthcare in Spain also subscribe to *Helicopteros Sanitarios*.

At this point I should point out that the ambulance service in Spain is not provided by the hospital and should you need to call an ambulance you will be asked to pay for the service. The service offered by the *Cruz Roja* (the Red Cross) can be expensive depending on the distance to the hospital. If you are dependent on the E111 form you may have to pay first and reclaim the cost so it does make a lot of sense to pay for the emergency service. The cost is minimal to ensure the great peace of mind which the service brings.

HEALTHCARE CASE HISTORIES

The coronary

One of the most dramatic examples of the life saving benefits of *Helicopteros Sanitarios* is shown in this case history. We have friends who live close by in a large house on the top of the hill. The sister of one of these friends lives about 10 minutes away in the valley on the edge of a golf course. Early on Christmas Day their father was staying in the sister's house. He became unwell and his daughter rang her brother to say that father looked as if he was having a coronary. Her brother rang the emergency number and by the time he drove down to his sister's house the helicopter ambulance service had landed on the golf course behind the house. Father was swiftly flown to the Costa del Sol hospital in Marbella and within 30 minutes of the first symptoms he was in intensive care in a room with only two patients. He

remained in hospital for 14 weeks so it really was a
serious coronary.

The gynaecological problem

Another friend has a minor gynaecological problem
which resulted in a visit to the GP. The GP diagnosis
suggested that a referral to a consultant would be
necessary. The choice was a health service appointment in
a week (our friend is an EU pensioner) or a private
appointment (which would cost around £40) the following
day. The second option was selected and the consultant
recommended hospital admission for a minor operation.
The date was set for the following week. The operation
went smoothly and the only complaint about the hospital
was that there was too much food offered during the
course of the day. The patient returned home after a few
days with a catheter still in place. Like many patients, she
fiddled around with the catheter and it came out. A call
to *Helicopteros* at 11 pm resulted in the ambulance
arriving within 20 minutes so that the doctor could
replace the catheter and they returned of their own
volition the next morning to check that everything was
satisfactory.

This case history is a perfect example of primary health
care, the hospital service and the emergency services
working well together with a mix of state and private
funding.

The broken leg

Another friend tripped in the garden one morning and hurt his leg. He nursed it all day and applied ice packs and all the other things you do for a sore leg. By the afternoon it was getting no better and in fact the swelling was becoming worse so he rang *Helicopteros*. Within 20 minutes they arrived and the doctor suspected a fracture, so our friend was taken to hospital in Marbella in the road ambulance. In fact the X-rays showed a fracture in two places and the treatment took about three hours.

At the end of the three-hour period the same emergency ambulance was waiting to take him back home again.

A case of food poisoning

This case history is actually my own. One Friday evening we went out for a meal. In the middle of the night I woke up with a very severe case of food poisoning. Even a glass of water would not stay in my stomach. I spent most of Saturday trying the various self medication remedies available for food poisoning but nothing was having any effect and I was beginning to panic a little. I was afraid of dehydration. I began to be concerned that it might be more than just simple food poisoning so I rang *Helicopteros*. Within 25 minutes the ambulance arrived and the doctor and nurse took a full medical history, made a full examination and treated me on the spot with emergency medication. They also reassured me that it was nothing more serious and left me with a prescription for more drugs from the pharmacy.

Following this experience, I was more than ever convinced that the subscription to the service was worthwhile.

Cancer

We have friends who live further along the coast who related this story to us. One of their neighbours who regularly spends six months of the year in Spain and six months in the UK had been feeling unwell so he took himself off to his Spanish GP. A whole battery of blood tests were performed and he returned to his GP a few days later for the results. The prognosis was not good and the GP gently told him that he had all the signs and symptoms of bowel cancer. The patient explained that he was returning to the UK the following day and that he would take the blood test results to his doctor back in England. The response of his Spanish GP was to ask if it was possible for him to change his travel plans because if he could, he could be admitted to hospital in Spain that very night for treatment. Needless to say he opted for immediate treatment in Spain rather than risk joining a waiting list in the UK.

OTHER HEALTHCARE SERVICES

Dentistry in Spain is just as good as it is in the UK and much cheaper. On average the cost of a trip to the dentist in Spain is about one third of the cost of a similar visit in the London area and the same type of dentistry is on offer. Such is the appeal of living and working in the more appealing environment of southern Spain that a large number of dentists from northern Europe have settled here and opened local practices. As a result you are likely to find that your chosen dentist could be Dutch, English or Scandinavian. The net result of this is that you will find a dentist who speaks fluent English so even if your Spanish is not fluent you do not need to worry.

There are also a large number of expatriates who can offer you other health interventions such as chiropody, osteopathy and a multitude of alternative therapies.

We are, of course, not the only animals to get sick. You may have pets. We now have two dogs in Spain, one we brought from England and one we rescued here from a local animal charity. We have found a super vet. He is Dutch and speaks good English and once more we have been pleasantly surprised at the low charges he makes for interventions which in the UK would have been much more expensive.

13

Are There Negatives?

Of course there are negatives – there always will be,
wherever you choose to live in the world – but I have to
say that this is probably one of the most difficult chapters
to write. Any discussion on negatives will inevitably
contain a certain degree of personal opinion and the
reader may actually decide that something which we
might consider to be a negative for us will be a
positive for them. So what are our negatives?

THE EXPATRIATE COMMUNITY

Of course, the expat community is not a negative in itself but I do have to say that it could be very easy to slip into a way of life which revolves around turning your little corner of Spain into the UK in the sun.

There are areas which are almost totally English speaking since so many expats live there. Some urbanisations are overwhelmingly English and the number of Spanish people owning property there can be lower than 10 per cent of the total. To me this is not living in Spain. I would prefer to feel that I was experiencing a different culture and a different attitude to life.

Not only does this apply to urbanisations, it also applies to complete areas of some towns, where you will find the shops are almost totally run by expats and the merchandise for sale has all been imported so that the shoppers can buy the English labelled goods they would have bought had they not left their home country. I personally find this very sad since many of the inhabitants of these areas and these communities are not living in Spain – they are here purely for the sun and the low cost of living.

We British often criticise the fact that there are immigrant communities in the UK who do not integrate fully. They have their own shops, cinemas and restaurants and they do not even try to learn English. This applies equally to many British immigrant communities in Spain.

I try to use my limited command of Spanish when I can and I have to say that it is improving all the time but I do find it sad when I visit my local resort area and try to order in Spanish only to have the waiter in the bar respond by asking if I could repeat my order in English, because he is English.

THE FREE HOLIDAY

Whenever you move to the sun and whatever country you move to it is amazing how many 'friends' you suddenly acquire. This phenomenon is something which needs to be nipped in the bud as soon as it starts. Of course it is wonderful to have visitors but if you are not careful it is very easy to end up feeling as if you are running a hotel and a taxi service all at the same time. You must try to differentiate between your very close friends, those who you really would want to come and stay in your home, and the others who see a free holiday on the horizon. For the latter group you should respond very quickly with an offer to find them accommodation for their holiday. In this respect we are now quite fortunate since we do have a second rental apartment so we can distinguish between house guests and those who really should rent from us if they want to come to Spain.

The question of transport is also something you have to consider. Where we live a car is essential to get around since we are one kilometre from the beach on high ground. As a result we now strongly advise anyone who comes for longer than a long weekend to rent a car. This means that they are independent, which really is very important. When you live here you do not go out every day to do tourist things and you do not eat out every evening. That is what you do on holiday so your guests need to have the freedom to do as they please and not make you feel guilty because you are not taking them around all the time.

Similarly even when you have house guests it can be a good idea to show them where the tea and coffee is so that they can help themselves rather than you having to turn yourself into a waiter, cook and maid for the duration of their stay.

HOLIDAYMAKERS

There are also possible irritations in the height of the holiday season if you live in an area where there are a large number of holidaymakers. They have paid good money to come here and some therefore think they have the right to make as much noise as they want with complete disregard to those people who live here all year round and for whom this is home.

Children are allowed to make as much noise as they wish around the swimming pool. Does it matter if they go around destroying the communal gardens? When we challenged one father about the behaviour of his children who were knocking all the flower heads off the plants with a stick we had the reply – 'I don't know what you are worrying about, the plants will grow again'!

The wonderful quietness in our urbanisation in the evening and overnight can be destroyed by people on holiday returning after a lot of alcohol at two in the morning and continuing to party on the terrace. It is amazing how easily noise travels when everything else is quiet.

This problem can be avoided if you are careful in your choice of property. If you do not want to live in a holiday area then do not buy in an urbanisation.

HOUSEHOLD BUILDING OR REPAIRS

It can be very comforting for the English speaking expatriate to hire the services of a fellow expat as a builder, decorator, plumber or electrician for renovation work or just general household repairs. At least you feel that the explanation of the work which needs to be done can be given clearly. Unfortunately there are very many examples of English builders ripping off their English expat clients. I would have to say that it is not always a deliberate rip off. The supplier is simply charging the hourly rate and the overall cost of the work were it to be done in the UK. Even the tradesman probably does not realise that the same work done by a local tradesman would be much cheaper. All this can be avoided by asking

for estimates from local Spanish contractors as well as
from your friendly expat.

STYLE OF CONSTRUCTION OF YOUR HOME

The style of construction rather than the quality of
construction can be a very real negative if you live here
all year round. Some of the minor irritations of an
apartment used only for holiday purposes can become
much more of a problem to the permanent resident.

Marble floors are wonderful for the heat of the summer
but can potentially cause noise problems. If your
neighbours have not fitted felt pads on chair or table legs
the noise made above, below or alongside your apartment
through the simple act of moving furniture may irritate
intensely. This is not helped by the fact that furniture
moving always seems to take place last thing at night. The
hard surfaces created by marble floors, painted walls and
very lightweight curtains can also cause problems with
television or hi-fi sound. We have a surround sound
system for our television but it is virtually impossible to
use it. The sub-woofer sits on the floor and the sound
from this speaker, even when played at low listening
levels, is absorbed into the structure of the building to the
extent that it might as well be in the living room of the
neighbours below us.

The methods used for construction of apartment blocks
can also lead to the very easy transmission of sound

through the building. A typical apartment block depends for its strength on a framework of concrete pillars and floors and the walls are simply added to this framework. Since the framework is common to every apartment the noise generated by major reconstruction work underway in another apartment, not necessarily immediately next door, can be transmitted through the entire structure and become a real nuisance if the building work goes on for many days.

Obviously these problems will not occur in a villa nor in an old town or village house but they could happen in modern townhouses. What you need to remember when selecting property is to think very carefully: is this property intended for permanent living or as a holiday home?

SHOPPING

Having lived in a big city we do find that shopping in Spain can be a bit limited in the area in which we live. There is no shortage of the shops you need for food or the everyday things of life but we do find that in a resort area the remainder of the shops can be a bit limited. To find the large department stores or smaller specialist shops we need to go to Marbella or Malaga to have a really good selection. There are out-of-town shopping centres springing up but unlike those in the UK they tend to be dominated by large electrical stores or DIY establishments rather than being a shopping centre in the true sense of the word. We do miss just going out to browse, especially in shops such as CD stores or bookshops. We now find ourselves browsing on the Internet.

THEATRE, CINEMA AND CONCERTS

Having lived in London we feel the absence of theatre, cinema and concerts. There is English theatre if you are prepared to drive along the coast to places like Fuengirola but that is quite a distance. There are cinemas in the larger towns which show films in English but I have to admit that we now tend to wait for those films we really want to see to be issued on DVD or video. In the large towns there are concerts but the scale is nothing like that we have been accustomed to.

I suspect that in the future we will make occasional forays back to the UK to stay with friends in London and while we are there we will gorge ourselves on the performing arts.

EXCHANGE RATES

The rate of exchange between sterling and the euro can be a positive or a negative if your income is in sterling. When we first moved here the euro was weak – our pounds could buy a lot of euros so prices seemed very cheap indeed. The exchange rate was a strong positive. As I write the pound has lost value against the euro and in real terms our income has dropped. For British expatriates who depend on a sterling income the entry of the UK into the Eurozone would be a very good move indeed. Whatever the exchange rate on entry this would be a fixed rate for the future and the expats would know exactly what their incomes would be and be able to budget accordingly.

It is, of course, possible to decide to put your investments into euro funds but when we moved the pound was very strong so this did not seem like a good idea. In retrospect perhaps we should have hedged our bets and mixed the investments. We do have one consolation, which is the fact that the income from our second property is in euros as is any capital appreciation which we might achieve. Perhaps this is as good a reason as any for investing money in property in Spain.

DEVELOPMENT

In many areas development is the real negative. The Costa del Sol is often referred to as the California of Europe and in many ways it is. We have the weather, we have the laid-back lifestyle but we also have a booming property market. Whenever this happens it attracts the developers and many others of the 'get rich quick' brigade.

The eastern end of the Costa del Sol was developed heavily several decades ago as far as the coastline is concerned and there is very little space on the coast to build any new property, so here the developers are moving further inland so long as the high ground on which they build has a view of the sea.

Between Marbella and Manilva and beyond it seems as if almost any piece of beach-front land is currently being built on. In a few years time it will probably be almost impossible to see the Mediterranean from the coast road. Hotels are being built together with apartment blocks and townhouses. Very few villas are under construction since a piece of land that could support a one million euro villa could probably support an apartment block whose total value would be far in excess of one million euros. Unfortunately many villas that were built along the coast road several years ago are now having their own views of the sea taken away. The developers are out to make as much profit as possible and many really do not care how much inconvenience they might be causing to existing residents so long as their bottom line is protected.

Unfortunately there is a lot of money to be made in property so the regulations are bent if not broken all the time. New planning permissions generally limit the height of a new structure in terms of the number of floors. However, the developers claim that the semi-underground carpark is not really a habitable floor and if the top floor apartments are two-floor duplexes then the top floor, the *attico*, is not really a floor either, it is part of the floor below. As a result planning permission for three floors results in a five-floor building. Many of the local town halls appear to be turning a blind eye to this flaunting of the planning permissions since every new apartment provides more potential income for the town hall.

The developers show no consideration to the people who live close to their building sites. The builders drive their heavy trucks over existing pavements and drains and in the process damage them. They clear sites for building work and drive the lorries full of the cleared earth through residential areas scattering mud or dust, depending on the time of year, over the existing roads.

Damage caused by the developers should be repaired and paid for by the same developers but they are not always too ready to co-operate. By using delaying tactics they may even hope that they can finish the development and move on, leaving the bills for the repairs to be picked up by the occupants of existing and new properties as an additional charge on the community fees. The inhabitants of an urbanisation have the responsibility of maintaining the roads in the development. This is not the responsibility of the town hall.

The salesmen, with one eye on their commission, tell prospective buyers that virtually all the properties have been sold, although this may not strictly be true. They have been sold to a speculator who has no intention of actually living in the property. All the speculator hopes to do is to resell (perhaps even before the property is complete) for a higher price. There are even adverts in English newspapers encouraging individuals to speculate on off-plan developments in Spain.

I am not against development. After all, had development stopped 20 years ago the apartment we purchased would not exist. Development is also the spur to improving local facilities and infrastructure and this can only be good in the long term. But development that flaunts planning regulations, and where buyers are given a misleading impression of their dream home, can be the cause of many problems for residents.

FINALLY . . .

These are the negatives as I see them to moving to Spain, but I believe the negatives are far outweighed by the positives (possibly with the exception of development which really needs to be considered if your lifestyle is going to be affected). So in summary, what are the positives?

◆ Warm, sunny weather.

◆ Better healthcare.

◆ Open spaces.

◆ Relaxed pace of life.

◆ Good public transport in developed areas.

- ◆ A large expatriate community if you want to be part of it.

- ◆ Better and healthier food.

- ◆ Relatively lower property costs.

- ◆ Lower local authority taxes.

14

Happily Ever After?

OUR FUTURE

It is always very difficult to foretell the future but we are
certain that ours will be in Spain, or at the very least it
will be outside the UK in a similar environment. Like
many others here who have become our friends, we are
not even considering a return to the UK since life is just
so much better here.

We are happy where we live at the moment but in the
longer term we will probably move to a property which is

more Spanish so that we really feel as if we are living in Spain. We want to have to learn to speak Spanish. We want to integrate into the Spanish way of life and have Spanish friends as well as English friends. We would like to live in a real Spanish town or village where we do not need to use the car every time we need to go out to buy something. We would like to be part of the community and enjoy the *ferias* and *fiestas* in the same way as the local Spanish population and not view them from the viewpoint of the tourist. We are unfortunately too old to consider buying a property with a bit of land which would allow us to live a life like that depicted in the television series, *The Good Life*, but were we ten years younger it would certainly be worth thinking about. The idea of self-sufficiency living on a little *finca* is a wonderful dream.

YOUR DECISION

Whether you are actively considering a move to Spain or have simply thought about it while visiting Spain on holiday, do think about it very seriously. Based on our experience, you are very unlikely to regret the move. If you make decisions based purely on the heart you might make a mistake but if you base your choice on both heart and head you are likely to be very happy in Spain.

CONCLUSION

I opened this book with a description of our old lives in

England and why we made the momentous decision to move to Spain. We know we have made the right decision but it is very interesting to compare our lives now compared with the lives we enjoyed (or thought we enjoyed) in our previous life.

Many of our friends probably thought we were very happy in that existence. At the time we thought we were happy too and it is only when we analyse the differences now that we realise that life in London was not as good as we thought.

We were both successful professionally and financially. We owned a large house. We had considerable disposable incomes and we lived up to those incomes. We thought we were very fortunate and we had worked hard over the years to reach that situation.

I appeared to have a glamourous job. I was jetting all over Europe or even further afield two or three times a month and building up frequent flyer rewards all the time which helped to subsidise our frequent holidays. My life revolved around travelling, business lunches or dinners and increasing stress, which was the catalyst that finally brought about the dramatic changes in our lives.

We enjoyed our shopping trips. Our clothes had to carry the right designer label. We indulged in 'retail therapy'. In reality we were trying to prove to everyone how successful we were through material possessions or conspicuous consumption.

On the whole material possessions do not impress people here. Individuals are accepted for who they are as a person not for their station in life. Just because someone lives in a very nice villa overlooking the sea you cannot jump to the conclusion that they are rich. They may have moved here many years ago when property was much cheaper. People generally have come to Spain to start a new life and the old life is rarely spoken of.

What a change has taken place in our lives since we arrived in Spain! Gone are the shopping trips. They are no longer necessary. Retail therapy is a thing of the past. All the designer clothes we brought with us are hanging in the wardrobe unworn apart from on the odd very special occasion. Since moving to Spain I have bought one pair of shoes and a few t-shirts. The dress code here is very relaxed indeed. In fact I have worn a tie once in 18 months.

Since I moved here I have not been on an aircraft once and I do not miss it one bit. We live in the sun so we certainly do not need to think about holidays in the sun. We have not even considered going back to the UK to visit since so many of our friends visit us here and we can catch up with the news.

Possibly for the first time in years we are really happy.

Stress is a distant memory and our lives are now much more relaxed. We can allow ourselves the luxury of waking up naturally rather than setting an alarm clock every morning. We have work to do looking after our second rental apartment. We are keyholders for some of the other apartments in the urbanisation for owners who do not live here all year round. I still do a bit of consultancy work linked to the industry I worked in for so many years. I do a little writing. Julian is now on the management board of our urbanisation with shared responsibility for the communal gardens.

Friends back in the UK have asked us whether we get bored in a semi-retired situation. We would have to say boredom is not in our dictionary. We see more friends here than we ever saw in London and we make more telephone calls. Often we wonder where the day has gone.

From spring to late autumn we have breakfast, lunch and dinner on the terrace – or for lunch we can drive down to the nearest beach restaurant and have a nourishing, inexpensive lunch enjoying the clear, fresh air and the view of the cobalt blue sea. Such a lunch is even possible in December or January. For most of the year the terrace doors are open throughout the day.

We do have less disposable income in Spain than we had in London but we do not need it. We have no debts and no mortgages so all we have to do is to pay the utility bills, buy clothes when we need them, and buy food.

Without debts it is amazing how little money one actually needs to live. With a bit more than the minimum amount of money one begins to live very well.

All in all, life now is so much better – when the sun shines almost every day you really do feel better. We reflect often on how wise our decision was to move to Spain, the land of 'blue drizzle'. If you are considering a similar move, I would encourage you to make the leap.

Recommended Reading

Andalucia by Michael Jacobs (1999, Pallas Guides).

Buy to Let in Spain by Harry King (2003, How To Books).

Buying a Home in Spain by David Hampshire (2nd edition 2000, Survival Books).

Buying a Property in Spain by Harry King (2002, How To Books).

Finca: Renovating an old farmhouse in Spain by Alec Fry (2003, Santana Books).

Gardening in Spain by Marcelle Pitt (1991, Santana Books).

Going to Live on the Costa del Sol by Tom Povan (2004, How To Books).

Going to Live in Spain by Harry King (2003, How To Books).

You and the Law in Spain by David Searl (2004, Santana Books).

CHOOSING A FOREIGN EXCHANGE COMPANY?
TRY CURRENCIES DIRECT

There has been a huge increase in the number of foreign exchange specialists who want to help you move your money to Spain. Deciding which one to use can be a daunting prospect but these simple guidelines should make the task a little easier.

◆ Select a company that has at least three years of audited accounts and is financially strong.

◆ Find out more information by doing a quick internet search on the company. Look out for whether they have won any awards or been recommended by a reliable source.

◆ Do not let a foreign exchange company pressurise you into doing a deal. Their job is to understand your requirements and to provide you with the information you need, not to hard sell and certainly not to make you trade until you are 100% happy.

◆ Ask what charges apply. If you are unsure, ask them to confirm in writing. You can really save money by using a well established, reputable foreign exchange company; not only through better rates but also as a result of lower transfer charges.

◆ Find out what foreign exchange buying options are offered. Some companies let you specify a rate at which you want to buy your currency (limit order) or fix a rate for up to 2 years (forward contract). These can be great tools to help you stick to your budget.

◆ Be aware that at present in the UK commercial foreign exchange is not an FSA regulated industry because it is not considered 'investment business'. Under the Money Laundering Regulations 2003, commercial foreign exchange companies are treated as "Money Service Businesses" which are covered by regulations administered by HM Customs & Excise.

Information provided by Currencies Direct.

www.currenciesdirect.com
Tel: 0845 389 1729
Email: info@currenciesdirect.com

Index

If you want to know how . . . to live and
work on the Costa del Sol

'The Costa del Sol is now one of the favourite destinations
for the British choosing to relocate to the sun and enjoy a
better quality of life. This book deals with the positives
and the negatives drawing from the experiences of people
who already live on the Costa del Sol.'

Tom Provan

Going to Live on the Costa del Sol
Tom Provan

This book covers vital issues such as education, healthcare
and taxes whilst offering advice on employment and self-
employment, property, day-to-day living, leisure activities
and legal issues.

If you are dreaming of a better lifestyle on Spain's
beautiful Costa del Sol, this fact-filled book will help you
make an informed decision about your change of lifestyle,
and ensure your dream does come true.

'Tom Provan . . . shares his experiences with advice on how
to settle in quickly to get the best from life in the sun.'
Living for Retirement

ISBN 1 85703 980 7

If you want to know how ... to buy to let in Spain

'Today's Spain is a young vibrant country. No land is so diverse or enjoys such an excellent climate. It has a strong personality, is full of rich traditions and has a totally unique culture. Spain is also Europe's biggest holiday playground, playing home to some 50 million foreign visitors each year who enjoy the delights of traditional family holidays on the Islands or Costas whilst many also explore the deep green pastures and cities of northern Spain, or sample the rural way of life.

Buy-to-let property owners are not commercial property developers since they wish to enjoy the benefits of their purchase too, but they do recognise the conundrum that a home is bought with the heart, a commercial property with the head and a buy-to-let property for fun and profit.'

Harry King

Buy to Let in Spain
Harry King

This inspiring book will help you fulfill your dream of a second home in Spain – and provide a steady income too. Buying a home in Spain is not expensive, but the procedures are very different and author Harry King uses his own experience to help you avoid the traps the unwary can fall into. Whether it is how to find a suitable property, how to deal with the Spanish conveyancing and letting system, or how to find tenants and run your property as a business, it's all explained in plain English.

ISBN 1 85703 890 8

If you want to know how . . . to start a new life in Spain

Spain has emerged as a prosperous and flourishing nation, attracting thousands of retirees and younger people from Northern Europe, who have made a conscious decision to move there.

Spain: Your Guide to a New Life
Harry King

This book looks at Spain's history, culture and customs. It is for foreigners at work, rest or play – enjoying retirement, taking a long term break or seeking employment and covers:

- The birth of a nation
- The economic miracle
- Development
- Security
- Diverse cultures, diverse languages
- Pros and cons of life in Spain
- Employment
- Getting the facts on retirement
- How Spain deals with 50 million visitors
- Knowing the essentials for a new life
- Buying a property
- Food and drink
- Traditional culture and New Spain
- Arts, literature, music and architecture
- Travel and communication

ISBN 1 84528 094 6

If you want to know how . . . to find your ideal property in Spain

How to Buy a Home in Spain
Harry King

Whether you want to buy for investment, as a holiday let or for permanent residence, Spain has much to offer. Buying a property there, whether it be a village house, city apartment or coastal villa, has its own features and author Harry King has all the information you need to make your purchase as easy as possible. In this book he leads you through the processes of:

- Deciding where to go and what to buy
- Buying off plan or resale
- Purchasing land and doing it yourself
- Searching for properties
- Taking care of your finances and the legal documentation
- Organising your move
- Dealing with taxation
- Settling in and enjoying your new lifestyle

ISBN 1 84528 086 5

If you want to know . . . about the law in Spain

There is little information available to help newcomers deal with Spanish Laws even though there is a real need for detailed information in a country where legal and practical contradictions appear commonplace.

Knowing the Law in Spain
Harry King

This book is not an academic description of the Spanish legal system. It is a practical guide to the most common applications of Spanish law affecting a foreigner who spends a considerable amount of time in Spain.
It covers:

- Your status as a European Union citizen
- Cash, credit and currency
- Buying, selling, letting or renting your property
- Customs control and consumer protection
- Working in Spain
- Personal taxation
- Buying, selling and running a car
- Birth, marriage, divorce and death
- Wills and inheritance tax

ISBN 1 84528 059 8

How To Books are available through all good bookshops, or you can order direct from us through Grantham Book Services.

Tel: +44 (0)1476 541080
Fax: +44 (0)1476 541061
Email: orders@gbs.tbs-ltd.co.uk

Or via our website

www.howtobooks.co.uk

To order via any of these methods please quote the title(s) of the book(s) and your credit card number together with its expiry date.

For further information about our books and catalogue, please contact:

How To Books
Spring Hill House
Spring Hill Road
Begbroke
Oxford OX5 1RX

Visit our web site at

www.howtobooks.co.uk

Or you can contact us by email at info@howtobooks.co.uk